Find Your Way to Freedom and Self-Determination

2nd edition & English translation of the German original version
(Revised edition, containing many new insights!)

Personal dedication to all readers:

Love never stops loving and will always be directed towards you, dear reader.
Lots of love from Margarete

This book did not undergo editing before being published, because I want to pass on my thoughts, insights and experiences in an unadulterated manner and without any perfectionism. Please forgive me if you find any mistakes in spelling, syntax, grammar, etc.

Description of the author:
In 1957, I was born as the fifth of nine children in a time after the Second World War, in which our parents were busy building up an existence. In 1977, I married the love of my life. Within five years after the wedding, life (love) gave us three daughters. Since then, I have become the happy grandmother of three grandchildren. In 2007, I left a very demanding "conventional" job where I could no longer express my social skills. Although I was already 50 years old, I completed a three-year training course to become a Shiatsu practitioner. During the training course I realised that I had finally found my vocation and that, in this profession, I could draw my creativity, vocations and talents from the abundance and fullness of the power source of light and love residing within myself. It was only late in my life that I realised that writing is another vocation of mine. In 2010 I opened my Shiatsu practice in my home town and, in the same year, I had my first book published by a publishing house.

Between 2010 and 2018 I wrote the manuscript for my second book titled "Selbstbestimmt und frei leben". On April 1, 2018, I self-published the first edition, consisting of 187 pages.
The second edition (translated into English under the title "Find Your Way to Freedom and Self-Determination") comprises 221 pages (and 198 pages in English) and contains many new insights and experiences.

Self-publisher: Margarete Neuhold
Hardegg 61
8454 Arnfels
Austria
https://www.margarete-neuhold.at

Printing: DMS DATA+MAIL Schinnerl GmbH (environmentally certified print shop)
Bookbinding: Hand-sewn binding with hardcover.

ISBN: 978-3-200-05554-4

Contents

Annexes:

Important information for my readers

In all my texts, "in the here and now" means: **"in the here and now" of being and living, in all cycles of being and living, in all places (environment, living space ...) of being and living, in all relationships, situations and communication within oneself, as well as between oneself and all beings and life itself, in singledom and coupledom, as well as in professional, business, leisure and social life.** After "in the here and now", I almost always leave out the preceding text.
World peace means peace in the world, in worlds and between worlds.

Important note: My stories and messages result from self-perceptions, my own life experiences and experiences with clients, and have no scientific background.

1.1. Draw "in the here and now", from the abundance and fullness of the power source of light and love residing within yourself

I have realised, I am aware and I experience again and again that like goes into resonance with like, that energies follow our expectations and that the **cause** of all natural phenomena, all elements (water, wood, fire, earth, metal/air)—which are the first natural phenomena and **which are present in all other natural phenomena**—as well as all beings (all humans, animals, plants, organisms ..., all microorganisms living in symbiosis in beings and all macroorganisms living in symbiosis with beings), i.e. **all beings and life itself, is love**.

In a state of physical, mental and spiritual (self-)awareness, (self-)perception and (self-)knowledge, realising that **love** is the **cause** of all beings and life itself, humans (all mammals) give birth to their children **by vibrating with the power of their own light and love**, without pain and while enjoying **full physical, mental and spiritual well-being as well as soul, family and world peace**.

Unfortunately, when I was pregnant with my first daughter, I imagined that I would have painful contractions during birth. For this reason, I went through 17 hours of painful contractions until my daughter was born after an episiotomy with severe subsequent pain. My second daughter was born in the care of a very sensitive midwife, completely without injuries and almost without pain. My third daughter came into the world with **power waves of light and love**, which flooded my body **self-dynamically** and powerfully, while we were enjoying **full physical, mental and spiritual well-being**. I experienced second stage contractions as an orgasm of my body, mind and soul.
Before the birth of my third daughter, I was fully aware that I was able to bring my child into the world **by vibrating with the power of my own light and love**. Although my youngest daughter is now 38 years old, pregnant women are still not prepared for a painless birth, because many people and unfortunately also many midwives and doctors have manifested "births with painful contractions" in their patterns of thought and belief. With this idea in mind, expectant mothers miss a **wonderful birth experience full of physical, mental and spiritual well-being**.

In the **biorhythmic ecological balance** and "in the here and now", **feminine and masculine forces** are comprehensively coordinated, **while nourishing the power of light and love**, and **in perfect harmony and balance** in all elements and beings—**in the water**, the kidney and bladder energy, **in the wood**, the liver and gall bladder energy, **in the fire**, the heart and small intestine energy, **in the secondary fire**, the cardiovascular and triple burner energy, **in the earth**, the stomach and spleen energy with the pancreas and **in the metal**, the lung and large intestine energy.
If, in each element (water, wood, fire, earth, metal/air) and "in the here and now", the masculine and feminine forces are **in harmony and balance, while nourishing the power of light and love, all elements (water, wood, fire, earth, metal/air) will automatically be comprehensively coordinated within themselves, as well as between themselves and all other elements, while nourishing the power of light and love—"in the here and now", in all beings and life itself**, in all beings (all humans, animals, plants, organisms ..., microorganisms living in symbiosis in beings and macroorganisms living in symbiosis with beings) and in all places (environment, living spaces) of their being and living, in the biorhythmic ecological balance, in a comprehensively

healthy growth and in the flow of being and living, where, in all energy flows, **exclusively love flows freely in a closed cycle**.
In this way, the **harmony** in and between the elements **that nourishes the power of light and love is reflected** "in the here and now", in beings and their living spaces, in one' identity- and individuality-based behaviour (that is identical to the love residing within oneself as well as specific to one's nature and that nourishes the power of light and love), in one's social, sexual, nature-specific, lifestyle-related, dietary, consumer and decision-making behaviour as well as in the balance of "giving and taking" for the purpose of maintaining and restoring **full physical, mental and spiritual well-being** and enjoying **soul, family and world peace within oneself, as well as between oneself and all beings and life itself**.

In a state of self-awareness, self-perception and self-knowledge, realising **that love is the cause of all beings and life itself**, all beings draw all-encompassing, pure and clear truth, wisdom and knowledge, all energies, vibrations and emotions of the **power of light and love** (such as being grateful, satisfied, in love, happy, motivated, enthusiastic, safe and cheerful), (self-)confidence, (self-)respect, happiness, calmness, health, self-safety, self-protection, etc. as well as all-encompassing and strong life, root, self-purifying, self-regenerating, self-transforming and self-healing powers **from the abundance and fullness of the power source of light and love residing within themselves** "in the here and now", with all-embracing gratitude, in a self-active, self-dynamic and automated way and **without consuming any resources**.

Vibrating with the power of their own light and love, all beings have, "in the here and now", completely unadulterated, pure, clear, strong and all-embracing **sensory perceptions** with all their completely healthy and strong senses (also with the third eye) and **intuitions** and a pure, clear, strong and all-embracing **instinct and mind**, which, like the elements, are **perfectly, and comprehensively, coordinated** in the biorhythmic ecological balance, "in the here and now" and **in harmony and balance, while nourishing the power of light and love** (right and left hemisphere of the brain, head and abdominal brain ...). "In the here and now", they act and react with **far-sightedness, insight and overview, with a good near and far view, with a good short- and**

long-term memory and in a "centred and concentrated" manner, while being identical to the love residing within themselves.

In this vibration all beings live out, while being strong in their midst, identical to the love residing within themselves and "in the here and now", **identity- and individuality-based behaviours that** are self-contained, identical to the love residing within themselves as well as specific to their nature and that **nourish the power of light and love** in their social, sexual, nature-specific, lifestyle-related, dietary, consumer and decision-making behaviour, in the balance of "giving and taking", with a strong spine (healthy back) and with a sense of justice, truth and equality that is **identical to the love residing within themselves** (love knows no evaluations) **for the purpose of maintaining and restoring full physical, mental and spiritual well-being and enjoying soul, family and word peace**, in the biorhythmic ecological balance and in a comprehensively healthy growth in the flow of being and living, where, in all energy flows, exclusively love flows freely in a closed cycle.

"In the here and now", they stand with both feet firmly on the ground which **vibrates from the power of light and love** and on which all elements are comprehensively coordinated and in harmony and balance, **while nourishing the power of light and love**. They only take, ingest and assimilate (also through their diet) **what is identical to the love residing within themselves**.

"In the here and now" and with a healthy approach to maintaining closeness and distance that is identical to the love residing within themselves, they disassociate themselves from nature-, gender- and society-specific evaluation-oriented systems built on illusions, delusions and hallucinations (that go deep into people's patterns of thought and belief and entail not only (self-)blocking and (self-)destructive behaviours in their social, sexual, nature-specific, lifestyle-related, dietary, consumer and decision-making behaviour, but also disharmonies and imbalances of "giving and taking", abuses of confidence, disregard for boundaries, competence withdrawals, paternalism and infantilising as well as physical, mental, spiritual, elemental and environmental contamination and injuries) as well as from blocking and destructive theories, views and opinions, manipulations and deceptions ... by communicating their own limits to the people around them and, on their part, clearly recognising and safeguarding all limits set by the people around them "in the here and now", with a pure and clear communication and while being identical to the love residing within themselves.

Vibrating with the power of their own light and love, all beings live with a free will, in self-determination and freedom, in the biorhythm of being and living, "in the here and now", in peace, harmony and balance within themselves, as well as between themselves and all beings and life itself, in the biorhythmic ecological balance, in a comprehensively healthy growth and in the flow of being and living, where, in all energy flows, **exclusively love flows freely in a closed cycle, in a completely autonomous, self-reliant and independent way** (independent of parents, children, life partners, friends, teachers ... and of all evaluation-oriented systems). Thus, "in the here and now", **exclusively love flows freely in a closed cycle** both within the generations and between the generations, with a healthy approach to maintaining closeness and distance that is **identical to the love residing within oneself**.
Autonomous, self-reliant and independent beings that vibrate with the power of their own light and love live "in the here and now", with a free will, in self-determination and freedom, in (self-)protection, in (self-)safety, in (self-)confidence, in (self-)respect, in self-awareness, in self-perception and in self-knowledge, are self-informed, self-organised, self-controlled, self-directed, self-guided, self-protected, self-confident, etc. and have a mindful and loving relationship with themselves as well as with all beings and life itself that is **identical to the love residing within themselves**, while maintaining the balance of "giving and taking" and enjoying **full physical, mental and spiritual well-being as well as soul, family and world peace**.
Thus, the mindful and loving relationship that is **identical to the love residing within oneself is reflected** "in the here and now" within oneself (in the body, mind and soul), as well as between oneself and all beings and life itself, in singledom and coupledom, as well as in professional, business, leisure and social life.

Symptoms of the body, mind and soul, disharmonies and imbalances (personal issues to work on) **within ourselves, as well as between ourselves and beings and life itself**, between ourselves and natural phenomena, elements (water, wood, fire, earth, metal/air) and beings (humans, animals, plants, organisms ..., microorganisms living in symbiosis in beings and macroorganisms living in symbiosis with beings) in being and living, in cycles of being and living, in places (environment, living spaces) of being and living, in relationships, situations and communication within ourselves, as well between

ourselves and beings and life itself, in singledom and coupledom, as well as in professional, business, leisure and social life, **draw our attention to personal issues within ourselves, as well as between ourselves and beings and life itself, and to their causes** (such as traumatic experiences with fears and shocks, mistrust, (self-)doubt, ingratitude, dissatisfaction, despair, insecurity, confusion, disorientation, envy, jealousy, anger, fury, hatred, aggressions, imperiousness, craving for power, possessiveness or addictions), to (self-)blocking and (self-)destructive manifestations, fixations and fanaticism built on illusions, delusions and hallucinations (that go deep into people's patterns of thought and belief and entail not only (self-)blocking and (self-)destructive social, sexual, nature-specific, lifestyle-related, dietary, consumer and decision-making behaviours, but also disharmonies and imbalances of "giving and taking", abuses of confidence, disregard for boundaries, paternalism and infantilising, deprivations of the right of decision-making, competence withdrawals, physical, mental, spiritual, elemental and environmental contamination and injuries, resource exploitations, etc.), to the **repeated seizure**, ingestion and assimilation (also through diet) of (self-)blocking and (self-)destructive energies, vibrations and emotions from external influences as well as to the **repeated entering into resonance** with such energies, vibrations and emotions coming from e.g. evaluation-oriented (power) systems which disseminate news and historical traditions, also via multimedia channels, for someone's own purposes and in a manipulated way.
In a state of (self-)awareness, (self-)perception and (self-)knowledge, realising that **love is the cause of all beings and life itself**, all beings, guided by truth, wisdom and knowledge, **recognise**, "in the here and now" and **based on the power source of light and love residing within themselves, personal issues and their causes** within themselves, as well as between themselves and beings and life itself, to which symptoms of their body, mind and soul, disharmonies and imbalances (**alarm signals**) "in the here and now" **draw their attention**.

Love, the cause of all beings and life itself, that is given by lovers reaches and suffuses "in the here and now" all beings and life itself—all natural phenomena, all elements (water, wood, fire, earth, metal/air), all beings (all humans, animals, plants, organisms ..., all microorganisms living in symbiosis in beings and all macroorganisms living in symbiosis with beings), the body, mind and soul, beings and life itself, all cycles of being and living, all places (environment, living spaces ...) of being and living, all relationships, situations and communication within oneself, as well as between oneself and all beings and life itself, in singledom and coupledom, as well as in professional, business, leisure and social life.

If **lovers give their love** to themselves as well as to all beings and life itself "in the here and now" and in a state of physical, mental and spiritual self-awareness, self-perception and self-knowledge of causes, while undergoing self-purifying, self-regenerating, self-transforming and self-healing processes, **the love given by lovers, the cause of all beings and life itself, will go, "in the here and now", into resonance with the love in all beings and life itself, and the love in all beings and life itself, the cause of all beings and life itself, will go into resonance with the love given by lovers**. **Love goes into resonance with love.**

By **going into resonance with love**, the cause of all beings and life itself, all beings involved in issues to work on, guided by truth, wisdom and knowledge, **recognise**, **"in the here and now"** and based on the **power source of light and love residing within themselves**, the **issues to work on and their causes** within themselves, as well as between themselves and beings and life itself.

As soon as beings have perceived and recognised personal issues and their causes consciously and **identically to the love residing within themselves**, they will detox, purify, declutter and cleanse themselves **"in the here and now"** from all (self-)blockages and (self-)destruction, from (self-)blocking and (self-)destructive parasite energies, vibrations and emotions and from occupation and domination by foreign souls with blocking and destructive foreign energies, vibrations and emotions. With a free will, in self-determination and freedom, in a self-convinced and determined way, with strong volition, resolution, decision-making power and (self-)persuasive power, with all-encompassing and strong self-purifying, self-regenerating, self-transforming and self-healing powers and **based on the power source of light and love residing within themselves, all beings involved in issues to work on comprehensively reconcile these issues and their causes "in the here and now"**—all causes of symptoms of the body, mind and soul, disharmonies and imbalances within themselves, as well as between themselves and beings and life itself, **coming from** the subtle and gross body (from each cell and from cellular consciousness, from the light body), from the mind (brain matrix, hard disk, head and abdominal brain), from the soul (soul matrix), from beings and life itself, from all cycles of being and living, from all places (environment, living spaces ...) of being and living, from all relationships, situations and communication within oneself, as well as between oneself and all beings and life itself, in singledom and coupledom, as well as in family, professional, business, leisure and social life,—**with the love residing within themselves and with the love between themselves and all beings and life itself and let these issues go "in the here and now", eliminating, resolving and deleting them and transforming them into "emptiness"**.

With energies, vibrations and emotions of the **power of light and love**, drawn "in the here and now" **from the power source of light and love residing within themselves**, all blocking and destructive energies, vibrations and emotions within oneself, as well as between oneself and all beings and life itself, **transform with the love** within oneself, as well as between oneself and all beings and life itself, **"in the here and now" into energies, vibrations and emotions of the power of light and love** (ingratitude into gratitude, dissatisfaction into satisfaction, mistrust and self-doubt into (self-)confidence, sadness into joy, disorientation into being self-oriented and self-informed, confusion into clarity, blindness and obfuscation into pure, clear and all-embracing vision with far-sightedness, insight and overview, unhappiness into happiness, insecurity into self-safety, defencelessness into (self-)protection ..., being outwardly oriented and in bondage to the outer world and being manipulated, remote-controlled, misprogrammed, dominated and occupied by the outer world into **living with a free will and in self-determination and freedom**, (self-)blocking and (self-)destructive behaviours caused by an imbalance of "giving and taking" into **identity- and individuality-based behaviours that are identical to the love residing within oneself as well as specific to one's nature and that nourish the power of light and love** in one' social, sexual, nature-specific, lifestyle-related, dietary, consumer and decision-making behaviour while maintaining the balance of **"giving and taking"**) **for the purpose of maintaining and restoring full physical, mental and spiritual well-being and enjoying soul, family and world peace**, in the biorhythmic ecological balance, in peace and harmony within oneself, as well as between oneself and all beings and life itself, in a comprehensively healthy growth and in the flow of being and living **that nourishes the power of light**

and love and where, in all energy flows, **exclusively love, the cause of all beings and life itself, flows freely in a closed cycle**.
As soon as **all personal issues and their causes** (all causes of symptoms of the body, mind and soul, disharmonies and imbalances) have been comprehensively reconciled "in the here and now" with the **love** residing within oneself, as well as between oneself and all beings and life itself, resolved and **transformed into emptiness or into love**, all symptoms of the body, mind and soul will regenerate and heal **in a self-dynamic and automated way** and without consuming any resources, "in the here and now", with pure, clear and all-encompassing truth, wisdom and knowledge, energies, vibrations and emotions of the **power of light and love** and strong and all-encompassing life, root, self-purifying, self-regenerating, self-transforming and self-healing powers drawn from the abundance and fullness of the **power source of light and love residing within oneself**; that is to say that all disharmonies and imbalances, **once comprehensively reconciled with the love within oneself, as well as between oneself and all beings and life itself, dissolve into love (into powerful vibrations of light and love)**.

After all-encompassing self-purification, -regeneration, -transformation and -healing, the body, mind and soul, beings and life itself, all cycles of being and living, all places (environment, living spaces ...) of being and living as well as all relationships, situations and communication within oneself, as well as between oneself and all beings and life itself, in singledom and coupledom, as well as in professional, business, leisure and social life, are "in the here and now", in the biorhythmic ecological balance, in peace and in harmony within themselves, as well as between themselves and all beings and life itself, in a comprehensively healthy growth and in the flow of being and living that **nourishes the power of light and love** and where, in all energy flows, **exclusively love flows freely in a closed cycle, while enjoying full physical, mental and spiritual well-being as well as soul, family and world peace**.
In this way, the macroorganism of beings and all microorganisms living in symbiosis within beings (microbiome) are—"in the here and now", **in clean biotopes, with a healthy body environment**, in the biorhythmic ecological balance, in a comprehensively healthy growth and in the flow of being and living—**perfectly, and comprehensively, coordinated, while nourishing the power of light and love**.

In the human macroorganism, there are about 100 times more symbiotically living microorganisms than human cells. Humans have about 22,000 (human) genes, the microorganisms living in symbiosis in our bodies have up to 3 million genes (source: "Warum nur die Natur uns heilen kann" [Why only nature can heal us] from Dr. med. habil. Dr. Karl J. Probst).
The interaction between the macroorganism and the symbiotically living microorganisms (microbiomes)—**in the biorhythmic ecological balance, in a comprehensively healthy growth and in the flow of being and living**—can only work if the microorganisms living in symbiosis in beings find **clean and healthy biotopes**.

In a state of self-awareness, self-perception and self-knowledge, knowing **that love is the cause of all beings and life itself**, all people (all beings) **draw, "in the here and now", their creativity, vocations and talents from the abundance and fullness of the power source of light and love residing within themselves** with all-embracing gratitude, in a self-dynamic, automated and self-active way and without consuming any resources.
Vibrating with the power of their own light and love, all people (all beings) **live out** their creativity, vocations and talents **"in the here and now"**, with **all-embracing** (self-)motivation and enthusiasm, **identically to the love within themselves, in a completely autonomous and self-reliant way, independently following the biorhythm of life, with a secure income and livelihood that are identical to the love residing within themselves, in the balance of "giving and taking"**, without resource exploitations, paternalism and infantilising, competence withdrawals, physical, mental, spiritual, environmental and elemental contamination and injuries ..., in the biorhythmic ecological balance, in peace and in harmony within themselves, as well as between themselves and all beings and life itself, in a comprehensively healthy growth and in the flow of being and living, where, in all energy flows, **exclusively love flows freely in a closed cycle, while enjoying full physical, mental and spiritual well-being as well as soul, family and world peace**.

Vibrating with the power of their own light and love and the love between themselves and all beings and life itself, all natural phenomena, all elements (water, wood, fire, earth, metal/air), all beings (humans, animals, plants, organisms ...), all beings and life itself are, **in the here and now, sealed with**

the power of light and love and fully protected, in (self-)safety and in (self-)protection, against blocking and destructive **energies** (such as parasites, pathogens, fungi, germs, viruses, bacteria, gluten, agglutinins, occupation and domination by foreign souls ...), **vibrations** (such as pathogenic and destructive high-frequency radioactive contamination, chemical (metal) contamination, magnetism, electromagnetic and digital (radio) microwaves attracted and stored by digital devices like smartphones and the like, the Internet, PCs, television ..., LED light sources and barcodes from satellites, radio masts, fibre optic cables, telephone and power lines, horizontal contamination, etc.) and **emotions** (such as fears and shocks due to traumatic experiences, mistrust, dissatisfaction, ingratitude, doubt, anger, fury, hatred, aggressions, envy, jealousy, despair, disorientation, obstinacy, stubbornness and blindness, unjustified judgmental criticism with justification demands, possessiveness, craving for power and imperiousness, addictions, etc.), against confrontations and going into resonance with blocking and destructive behaviours in their social, sexual, nature-specific, lifestyle-related, dietary, consumer and decision-making behaviour due to an imbalance of "giving and taking", against being outwardly oriented, being in bondage to the outer world, being manipulated, remote-controlled and misprogrammed by the outer world, being stuck in roles of victim and perpetrator and being the vicarious agent for power systems and power seekers, against group pressures, energy thieves, raids, attacks, vandalism ..., against manipulations and deceptions of evaluation-oriented systems in (fear-inducing) representations serving someone's own purposes (which are spread via multimedia channels, such as the Internet, TV, radio, newspapers, magazines, books and stage performances, as well as in advertisements, (feature) films, news and historical traditions, against nightmares with anxiety attacks and insomnia, against addictions ..., against diseases, depressions, manias, strokes of fate, accidents, (self-imposed) pain and suffering, (self-)punishment compulsions, (self-)marginalisation, feelings of guilt and a bad conscience, accusations, restrictions of motion and immobility, rootlessness ... and, in the worst case, against murder and suicide out of desperation and a sense of hopelessness or because of possessiveness, craving for power and imperiousness while being stuck in roles of victim and perpetrator, in short, against all (self-)blockages and (self-)destruction.

1.2. Dissociation and distancing

In a state of self-awareness, self-perception and self-knowledge, realising that **love is the cause of all beings and life itself, lovers give, in the here and now, love to themselves as well as to all beings and life itself. They feel sympathy**, but **do not go into resonance** with fear-inducing energies, suffering, pain, untruths, false theories and opinions, etc. (blocking and destructive energies, vibrations and emotions) from external influences. They do not take over any burdens from patients, clients, life partners, relatives, friends, etc. (people or other natural phenomena, beings and life itself), since that would entail a disregard for boundaries with competence withdrawal and paternalism.

Although I perceive disharmonies and imbalances and often unpleasant symptoms of the body, mind and soul within myself, as well as between myself and beings and life itself, I **exclusively go into resonance**, "in the here and now", with energies, vibrations and emotions **of the power of light and love**, with strong and all-encompassing life, root, self-purifying, self-regenerating, self-transforming and self-healing powers, with the pure, clear, all-encompassing and completely unadulterated truth and wisdom and with the pure, clear and all-encompassing knowledge drawn **from the power source of light and love residing within myself and from the power sources of light and love residing within beings and life itself** in my partner relationship, family, professional, business, leisure and social life.
Ever since I started eating life and root force-strengthening, seasonal and regional organic food in seasons' biorhythm without agglutinins, gluten, yeast, animal ingredients and sugar and ever since I started avoiding manipulations and deceptions from multimedia channels, my sensory perceptions (seeing, hearing, smelling, tasting, feeling, thinking ...), my intuition, my instinct and my mind have been purer, clearer, more intense, stronger and more comprehensive.

1.3. Love never stops loving

Love, which never stops loving, is the cause of beings and life itself. Love is, "in the here and now", always directed towards all beings and life itself. It is an inexhaustible power source of light and love within and for all beings and life itself, and does not consume any resources.

In a state of self-awareness, self-perception and self-knowledge, realising that **love is the cause of all beings and life itself**, beings draw, "in the here and now", pure, clear and all-encompassing truth, wisdom and knowledge, all energies, vibrations and emotions of the **power of light and love**, pure, clear, strong and all-encompassing life, root, self-purifying, self-regenerating, and self-healing powers ... **from the inexhaustible power source of light and love residing within themselves**.

Love, like the soul, the spirit and the aura, is a subtle energy. There are no evaluations, no conditions, no judgments, **no beginning and no end** in **love, the cause of all beings and life itself**, and, as everywhere in the world of subtle matter, there are no time or space limitations in love, but only the **"here and now"**.
All natural phenomena, all elements (water, wood, fire, earth, metal/air), all beings (humans, animals, plants, organisms ..., all microorganisms living in symbiosis in beings and all macroorganisms living in symbiosis with beings), all beings and life itself, feminine and masculine forces ... are **neither superior nor inferior in love**.

For **maintaining and restoring the biorhythmic ecological balance** in peace and in harmony within themselves, as well as between themselves and all beings and life itself, in a comprehensively healthy growth and in the flow of being and living, where, in all energy flows, **exclusively love flows freely in a closed cycle**, all natural phenomena, all elements (water, wood, fire, earth, metal/air), all beings (humans, animals, plants, organisms ..., all microorganisms living in symbiosis in beings and all macroorganisms living in symbiosis with beings), **all beings and life itself complete tasks that are identical to the love residing within themselves**.

Beings can only complete these tasks while being **identical to the love residing within themselves** if they draw, **"in the here and now"**, their creativity, vocations and talents from the abundance and fullness of the **power source of light and love residing within themselves** and **live out identity- and individuality-based behaviours that are identical to the love residing within themselves as well as specific to their nature and that nourish the power of light and love** in their social, sexual, nature-specific, lifestyle-related, dietary, consumer and decision-making behaviour and **in the balance of "giving and taking" for the purpose of maintaining and restoring full physical, mental and spiritual well-being and enjoying soul, family and world peace**.
Predators equipped with canine teeth and/or claws or talons remove sick and weak animals from the healthy ecological balance. Insects eliminate diseased plants which are not (no longer) in the biorhythmic ecological balance and in a comprehensively healthy growth. Cats help to prevent mouse plagues ...
Dead materials such as dead leaves, wood, plants ... are food sources and habitats of many living beings (macroorganisms and microorganisms), which decompose dead organic matter back to earth **without forming rot**. The king of the macroorganisms in the earth is the earthworm, which eats organic material, digests it (decomposes it to earth) and provides the plants with its wonderful earthworm humus in a very short time.
Lactic acid bacteria, photosynthetic bacteria and fungi such as yeast fungi attack dead organisms in keeping with their mission and decompose these organisms (dead matter) in a **decay process** (rotting process) back to earth. Undigested food in the intestines of humans is also attacked by lactic acid bacteria, photosynthetic bacteria and fungi and begins to decompose in the intestines (comprehensively explained in the nutrition section of this book).
"In the here and now", for **maintaining and restoring** the biorhythmic ecological balance in peace and in harmony within themselves, as well as between themselves and beings and life itself, in a comprehensively healthy growth and in the flow of being and living, where, in all energy flows, **exclusively love flows freely in a closed cycle**, humans have **no direct task** to complete, such as eating killed animals. For meat digestion, humans have neither suitable teeth nor suitable digestive conditions. Furthermore, neither their saliva nor their digestive juices contain suitable **microorganisms living in symbiosis there**, which, similar to soil life in the earth, would be able to

decompose the meat **without forming rot (decay)** and make its nutrients available to the macroorganism.
Behaviours that are not identical to the love residing within oneself in one's social, sexual, nature-specific, lifestyle-related, dietary, consumer and decision-making behaviour and that entail not only disharmonies and imbalances of "giving and taking", but also abuses of confidence, disregard for boundaries, paternalism and infantilising, deprivations of the right of decision-making, competence withdrawals, physical, mental, spiritual, elemental and environmental contamination and injuries, resource exploitations, interventions preposterous to nature in natural phenomena (including genetic manipulation), etc. in elements (water, wood, fire, earth, metal/air), in beings (humans, animals, plants, organisms ..., microorganisms living in symbiosis in beings and macroorganisms living in symbiosis with beings) as well as **in life itself** block and destroy the biorhythmic ecological balance, the comprehensively healthy growth in the flow of being and living and, subsequently, the **physical, mental and spiritual well-being in soul, family and world peace** within oneself, as well as between oneself and all beings and life itself.

1.4. Self-healing with the power source of light and love residing within yourself

You can **regenerate yourself energetically and heal yourself** through the abundance and fullness of the **power source of light and love residing within yourself**—without any side effects. In the case of symptoms, disharmonies and imbalances, I place one hand below the navel and one hand above the navel or on the affected areas (chakras, acupuncture points, muscles, organs, sensory organs ...). Afterwards, for self-purification, self-regeneration, self-transformation and self-healing, I draw, with all-embracing gratitude and **without consuming any resources**, from the abundance and fullness of the **power source of light and love residing within myself**.
After a bronchitis with strong symptoms I got myself, "in the here and now", with all-embracing gratitude and while meditating, pure, strong and all-encompassing self-purifying, self-regenerating, self-healing, life and root

powers, energies, vibrations and emotions of the **power of light and love**, completely pure, clear and all-encompassing truth, wisdom and knowledge from the **power source of light and love residing within myself** for **recognising the causes of my symptoms** and for **resolving issues** within myself, as well as between myself and **beings and life itself, "in the here and now" and in an all-encompassing and reconciling manner**.

As soon as all personal issues and **their causes** have been comprehensively reconciled "in the here and how" with the love within oneself, as well as between oneself and all beings and life itself, **resolved** and transformed into **emptiness** or into energies, vibrations and emotions of the **power of light and love**, all symptoms of the body, mind and soul will heal "in the here and now" with self-purifying, self-regenerating, self-transforming and self-healing power drawn from the **power source of light and love residing within oneself**; that is to say that all disharmonies and imbalances within oneself, as well as between oneself and beings and life itself, once comprehensively reconciled, dissolve "in the here and now" **into love (into powerful vibrations of light and love)**.

After I had gone **into resonance** with the natural inorganic sulphur power in a meditation for intestinal repair and cleansing, without having taken the substance, I had to spend half an hour on the toilet after only five minutes because my intestine thoroughly detoxified and purified itself.

Due to the antibacterial effect of coconut oil I practised oil pulling in the morning, and, in addition, I took one to two teaspoons of virgin organic coconut oil every day until full healing occurred. I also went **into resonance** with the healing powers of self-collected organic herbs (sage, thyme, mallow, ribwort plantain, yarrow ...) in teas and many self-healing powers within me became active. I allowed myself sufficient time and rest for regeneration and healing so that all symptoms could heal. I also took a lot of liquid (clean and pure water with a good pH value) and inhaled a lot of clean and fresh forest air by taking long walks in the forest.

In a state of physical, mental and spiritual awareness, realising that **love is the cause of all beings and life itself, the body, mind and soul regenerate and heal** in a self-dynamic and automated way when being in deep relaxation and especially in deep sleep before midnight, **drawing from the abundance and fullness of the power source of light and love residing within themselves**. One hour of sleep before midnight has the same recuperative effect as three hours of sleep after midnight.

Harmonisation of the elements

In the morning or in the evening, before I fall asleep, I place my hands in the hara (upper and lower abdomen) and harmonise **“in the here and now” all elements and their elemental energy flows** within myself, as well as between myself and all beings and life itself, and in all places (environment, living spaces) of being and living. Afterwards, I direct **my love** “in the here and now” towards myself as well as towards all beings and life itself with the idea that my **love** goes **into resonance** with the **love** in all beings and life itself and that the **love** in all beings and life itself goes **into resonance** with my **love** and that the love given by me **is reflected “in the here and now” within myself, as well as between myself and all beings and life itself, while we are all enjoying full physical, mental and spiritual well-being as well as soul, family and world peace**. (Meditations can be found in the annexe.)

2.1. Why people do not (any longer) live their lives identically to the love residing within themselves

If people are outwardly oriented and, in the outer world, in bondage to nature-, gender- and society-specific evaluation-oriented religious, family, social or political systems, they are often manipulated, remote-controlled and misprogrammed by these systems and by people living in these systems, acting as vicarious agents and stuck in roles of victim and perpetrator of such systems (not only consciously but also unconsciously).
By repeatedly going **into resonance** with (self-)blocking and (self-)destructive energies, vibrations and emotions from external influences, such as (self-)blocking and (self-)destructive social, sexual, nature-specific, lifestyle-related, dietary, consumer and decision-making behaviours caused by an imbalance of “giving and taking”, abuses of confidence, disregard for boundaries, competence withdrawals, paternalism and infantilising, deprivations of the right of decision-making, physical, mental, spiritual, environmental and elemental contamination and injuries, resource exploitations ..., they adopt, influenced by the outer world, (self-)blocking and (self-)destructive behaviours with nature-, gender- and society-specific evaluation-oriented patterns of

thought and belief built on illusions and delusions—behaviours that they also manifest in their patterns of thought and belief and in their family system.
Evaluation-oriented systems, people living in such systems and people who are in bondage to such systems or have become dependent on such systems believe that humans can rule over and control other beings (other humans, animals, plants, organisms ...), elements (water, wood, fire, earth, metal/air), beings and life itself as superior "master beings". Such people either take on a subordinate role to power seekers and power systems and, consciously or unconsciously, become their vicarious agents or try to come to power themselves in these systems with money, possessions and wealth and/or with manipulations and deceptions in (fear-inducing) representations serving their own purposes because they want to rule over and control beings and life itself. From the outer world and from what they ingest, take and assimilate (also through their diet and from the multimedial world ...), they repeatedly receive energies, vibrations and emotions which are in line with the (self-)blocking and (self-)destructive manifestations, fixations and fanaticism within themselves and satisfy addictions within themselves.
By repeatedly **going into resonance** with blocking and destructive energies, vibrations and emotions from external influences, they remain, **like in a spiral**—without far-sightedness, insight and overview and outwardly oriented in (self-)blocking and (self-)destructive manifestations, fixations or fanaticism, with (self-)blocking and (self-)destructive behaviours, with disharmonies and imbalances of "giving and taking" and increasingly dependent on addictions—externally remote-controlled and misprogrammed victims of manipulation and deception, **caught up within themselves**.
In many cases, such life patterns (manifestations) are already brought along with incarnations in families and are lived (out) through many generations in (family) systems. If, through many generations, the same diseases, strokes of fate or accidents and even similar murders and suicides ... occur again and again in families, the causes are very rarely genetically inherited, but rather the consequences of (self-)blocking and (self-)destructive behaviours in people's social, sexual, nature-specific, lifestyle-related, consumer and decision-making behaviour, which entail disharmonies and imbalances of "giving and taking" and which have again and again become "(family) traditions" in family systems—also among descendants.

Those who are strongly outwardly oriented, in bondage to the outer world and manipulated, remote-controlled and misprogrammed by the outer world can often no longer **perceive love as the cause of all beings and life itself** within themselves, as well as between themselves and all beings and life itself. These people seek truth, wisdom, knowledge and healing in vain in the outer world, in many books, magazines, newspapers, lectures by "experts", religious and other systems, etc. instead of drawing pure, clear, all-encompassing and completely unadulterated truth, wisdom and knowledge **from the abundance and fullness of the power source of light and love residing within themselves**. Such people are often ungrateful, confused, irritated, disoriented ... and, despite material wealth, often unhappy and dissatisfied, because they can no longer see and perceive the **gifts of life** (also the gift of **love** within themselves, as well as between themselves and all beings and life itself) "in the here and now". Although they have often consumed and exploited their own resources and those of the people around them or let themselves be exploited, and although unpleasant and painful symptoms of the body, mind and soul, disharmonies and imbalances in relationships, situations and communication within themselves, as well as between themselves and beings and life itself, become stronger and stronger and increasingly intolerable, they often don't let go of the (self-)blocking and (self-)destructive manifestations, fixations or fanaticisms that have been manifested—and are still manifested—within themselves and their (family) systems as well as of "disease-causing" addictions because they have become heavily dependent on addictions, because they want to increase their possessions and material wealth more and more, adapting it to the latest "trend", because they want to have their partner, family, friends, business, employees, the people ... under "their sole control", because they want to dominate the "market", the "world", **all beings and life itself** and decide on and control all beings and life itself or because they want to live out and spread religious fanaticism.
Those who are in bondage to the outer world, evaluation-oriented, caught up in perfectionism and within themselves, manipulated, remote-controlled and misprogrammed by the outer world often prefer to remain "in self-deception" in the victim role (especially in material wealth) and continue to fake a perfect world until total collapse occurs, instead of taking the many alarm signals seriously and getting out of (self-)blockages and (self-)destruction "in the here and now".

Those who are addicted to recognition and attention will always place themselves "in the centre" on the stage of life. Even when having reached the autumn of their lives, these people often do not withdraw voluntarily to leave their place on the stage or position to younger people (their descendants), which would be in line with the biorhythm of their being and living. In these cases, symptoms such as tinnitus, metabolic, cardiovascular, cancer and joint diseases, manias, depressions and Parkinson's disease draw these people's attention **not only to a behaviour that is not identical to the love residing within themselves but also to the exploitation of resources**.

The **reasons** why creativity, vocations and talents are not drawn in a self-aware, self-recognised and self-perceived manner from the abundance and fullness of the **power source of light and love residing within oneself** and why creativity, vocations and talents are not lived out in the biorhythmic ecological balance, in peace within oneself, as well as between oneself and all beings and life itself, in a comprehensively healthy growth, in the flow of being and living where, in all energy flows, **exclusively love flows freely in a closed cycle**, in the balance of "giving and taking" and with an income and livelihood that are **identical to the love residing within oneself**, are often **loss of identity and individuality** due to strong outward orientations as well as personal issues that are not yet resolved and their causes within oneself, as well as between oneself and beings and life itself. Another reason is that the **process of cutting the cord** in the biorhythm of being and living for attaining a **level of independence and self-reliance that is identical to the love residing within oneself** is not yet completed.

In many cases, people only allow changes (in attitudes, views, etc.) to occur in social, sexual, nature-specific, lifestyle-related, dietary, consumer and decision-making behaviour within themselves and within their (family) systems when, in spite of symptom treatments repeatedly drawn from the outer world, the physical and psychological distress caused by pain and suffering has become unbearable or when their relationships, situations and communication within themselves, as well as between themselves and beings and life itself, in singledom and coupledom, as well as in family, professional, business, leisure and social life, are almost destroyed due to disharmonies and imbalances.

In desperate, hopeless and painful situations, some people are willing to **let go** of (self-)blocking and (self-)destructive behaviour with disharmonies and imbalances of "giving and taking" as well as of addictions, or **not to allow them to continue**.
However, in the long run, such people only live out **identity- and individuality-based behaviours that are identical to the love residing within themselves as well as specific to their nature and that nourish the power of light and love** while maintaining the harmony and balance of "giving and taking" for the purpose of maintaining and restoring full physical, mental and spiritual well-being and enjoying soul, family and world peace when they are **convinced** of these behaviours **themselves**.
If, during their regeneration and healing processes, people have not **recognised** the **causes** of personal issues, symptoms of the body, mind and soul, disharmonies and imbalances within themselves, as well as between themselves and beings and life itself, **for themselves** and "in the here and now", they will find it very difficult to find their **identity- and individuality-based behaviour that, in the balance of "giving and taking", is identical to the love residing within themselves as well as specific to their nature and that nourishes the power of light and love**.
Unfortunately, they will often live out the (self-)blocking and (self-)destructive "old, familiar and traditional (family) behaviours" (that are manipulated, remote-controlled and misprogrammed by the outer world and manifested within themselves) again, especially due to group pressure, as soon as pain, movement restrictions, etc. (symptoms of the body, mind and soul) have subsided after drug treatments (symptoms are suppressed) or after having changed (self-)blocking and (self-)destructive behaviours for a short time until the symptoms subsided.
With the (self-)blocking and (self-)destructive behaviour which is still manifested within themselves and with disharmonies and imbalances of "giving and taking", they burden themselves and the people around them again until unpleasant physical and psychological symptoms, disharmonies and imbalances send out **alarms** again.
If the body, mind and soul are confronted again and again with (self-)blocking and (self-)destructive behaviours, with disharmonies and imbalances of "giving and taking", abuses of confidence, disregard for boundaries, paternalism and infantilising, deprivations of the right of decision-making, competence

withdrawals, physical, mental, spiritual, environmental and elemental contamination and injuries, resource exploitations ... in victim and/or perpetrator roles, people (all beings) will die before their time from incurable diseases or from the consequences of accidents, because they are no longer in (self-)safety and (self-)protection due to their behaviour.

If relationships, situations and communication within oneself, as well as between oneself and beings and life itself, are again and again burdened with (self-)blocking and (self-)destructive behaviours in one's social, sexual, nature-specific, lifestyle-related, dietary, consumer and decision-making behaviour, entailing not only disharmonies and imbalances of "giving and taking", but also abuses of confidence, disregard for boundaries, paternalism and infantilising, deprivations of the right of decision-making, competence withdrawals, resource exploitations, physical, mental, spiritual, environmental (contamination of the environment and living space) and elemental contamination and injuries, unjustified judgmental criticism with demanded justifications, etc., relationships in singledom and coupledom, as well as in family, professional, business, leisure and social life, will break up.

2.2. Protect yourself from manipulation and deception

People who are strongly outwardly oriented and in bondage to the outer world and who have stopped drawing energies, vibrations and emotions of the power of light and love, strong and all-encompassing life, root, self-purifying, self-regenerating, self-transforming and self-healing powers as well as pure, clear and all-encompassing truth, wisdom and knowledge from the abundance and fullness of the **power source of light and love residing within themselves** "in the here and now" are, due to their **loss of identity and individuality**, often victims of manipulation and deception who are stuck in roles of victim and perpetrator and who are remote-controlled, other-directed and misprogrammed by the outer world.

Contraceptive methods

Contraception with the pill feigns pregnancy for women and often has serious consequences for the body, mind and soul. An acquaintance of mine has taken the pill for more than 20 years, although she was a smoker, and suffered a heart attack at the age of only 45. Women who take hormones from the outside via the pill or a hormone IUD no longer have a natural hormonal balance and a natural menstrual period. Hormones supplied from the outside cause menstrual bleeding to be very weak and very short or to stop altogether. Many, often still very young, clients of mine have said goodbye to the "pill" due to physical and psychological symptoms (extreme discomfort) or had the hormone IUD removed. After they were able to detoxify and purify themselves and release accumulated emotions with their natural menstrual bleeding and their blood received a monthly fresh cell cure due to their natural bloodletting, they felt comfortable in their body again. Psychological symptoms and blocked sexual behaviour, such as listlessness, extreme sexual desire and sexual serving, also resolved themselves completely with an uninfluenced natural monthly cycle. I was shocked when a very young client (still without children) told me that she had been given the 3-month injection by her gynaecologist as a method of contraception.

Hair dyeing and more

Young people usually dye their hair due to group pressure or because their **identity and individuality** have not yet consolidated. Older people usually do this because they are strongly outwardly oriented and in bondage to the outer world as well as obsessed with youth (wanting/having to look "young" forever) and because they follow a fashion trend out of group pressure.
Through the use of chemicals (ammonia, hydrogen ...) in hair dyeing, especially during bleaching, important vital functions of the hair are paralyzed. Every living, healthy hair is a transmitter and receiver; it transmits information from the environment into our consciousness and draws our attention to dangers. Animals also orient themselves with their whiskers. A cat without whiskers is no longer able to catch mice because it is disoriented without whiskers.

Chemically treated hair is energetically dead and can neither receive nor transmit information. With limited sensory perception, beings can no longer orient themselves comprehensively. Thus, they are no longer in the all-encompassing (self-)protection and the all-encompassing (self-)safety against blocking and destructive energies, vibrations and emotions from external influences.
During hair dyeing, the flame of life that rises from the crown chakra is damaged or, in the worst case, extinguished. The crown chakra with the flame of life in the centre of the head is the **information centre** for the pure, clear and all-encompassing truth and wisdom and for the pure, clear and all-encompassing knowledge **from the power source of light and love residing within oneself**, which is, after hair dyeing, no longer available "online" and "free to the door" **from the abundance and fullness of the power source of light and love residing within oneself**. Loss of identity and individuality, weak powers of will, decision, resolution and persuasion, lack of energy ... are often the consequences.
The crown chakra with the flame of life can only regenerate in a clean and healthy environment (living space) and only when the hair is no longer chemically treated.
With regenerated and healthy hair, sensory perceptions through the hair are possible again. The destroyed hair, which can no longer be healthy, should be cut off after the healthy regrowth. Non-dyed natural and white hair fulfil all life functions and are a mirror of lived **identity and individuality**.

Piercings block or interrupt the free-flowing energy flows of the power of light and love. Please protect your children and especially your babies from earlobe piercing for earrings; both adults and children are subject to group pressure here. Piercing the earlobe destroys important acupuncture points and interrupts the free flow of energies.
Since the skin is an important sensory, detoxifying, purifying and respiratory organ, tattoos are **completely out of place** there.

2.3. Protect yourself from remote-controlled consumer behaviour

A client, who was an authorised signatory in an advertising company many years ago, told me that she had received insider knowledge during a training course on the introduction of barcodes. Digitalized barcodes make it possible to collect money with digital check-outs. However, they are also intended to trigger increased consumer behaviour among consumers and, with this function, increase sales. During payment, barcodes on goods or their packaging are charged with electromagnetic digital (radio) microwaves. At the same time, they trigger multimedia online booking in the accounting department (sales, inventory ...) of the shop and the company. Meanwhile it is assumed that people's consumer behaviour can be interrogated by barcodes for targeted advertising use with the (wireless) Internet or by means of satellites via activated digital devices (smartphones, PCs, televisions, electronic devices ...) in the house or in the living environment. This should be possible with strong electromagnetic digital radio microwaves with a longer range, similar to the payment of goods. If this has become possible and is applied, people who do not destroy barcodes and who have (permanently) activated the (wireless) Internet and digital devices are increasingly exposed to strong electromagnetic digital radio microwave emissions. When my husband recently bought a new colour printer, there was even a wireless Internet installed and activated in that printer. We immediately disabled the wireless Internet in the printer.
Shortly after barcodes and QR codes were introduced, the prognosis made during the introduction of barcodes has come true. In many families (from the grandparents to the grandchildren) shopping has more and more become a favourite pastime. Even on weekdays it is often difficult to get a parking space for your car in shopping malls that have sprung up like mushrooms.
I destroy all barcodes and QR codes after paying on newly purchased goods or on their packaging, if possible, before packing them into the car or at home, by cutting them with scissors, or scraping them off the labels on glass bottles. I do the same with receipts. Since I also destroyed all the old barcodes and QR codes on glasses, boxes and invoices as well as on goods that were often bought a long time ago, and since I cleared out my linen cupboard and

wardrobe, the cellar and attic and all the storerooms, I feel much more comfortable and free in my house. I even found two barcodes hidden under the battery of my key mobile phone.
Membership cards of companies, which are scanned when paying for goods at their points of sale, are also digitally and electromagnetically charged afterwards. They provide the company with important information on the consumer behaviour of its "member customers". For this reason, I cancelled all memberships in companies and shops, disposed of the cards and had my data deleted from the systems.

2.4. Perceive, recognise and become aware of the causes of symptoms on your own

Recently, I fortunately have been meeting more and more people who, often after years of orthodox medicine and alternative treatments, have recognised for themselves that the **causes** of creeping or suddenly occurring, often extremely severe, rheumatism-like joint and muscle pain and headaches, cardiovascular problems, dizziness, migraine attacks, sleeplessness, energy loss, nosebleeds ... can also be **electromagnetic** microwaves with an often very strong magnetism, such as e.g. microwave ovens and induction ovens operated with **magnetism**, induction dishes with a magnetic core, electronic household appliances, remote-controlled toys ..., **digital** (light) radio microwaves from digital devices such as smartphones and the like, the Internet, televisions, PCs ... (which get radio microwaves, often in a very high frequency, out of radio masts and satellites) and chemical or radioactive environmental pollution, multimedia exposure ... from their living environment.
With activated digital devices such as mobile phones, the (wireless) Internet, radios, television sets, PCs, navigation systems, sports watches ... **electromagnetic** and digital (radio) microwaves are brought into the house, the car ... (to oneself) from radio masts, satellites, fibre optic cables, telephone and power lines. When natural phenomena are exposed to **electromagnetic** and digital (radio) microwaves, heavy metal pollution, radioactive radiation ... without protection, high frequencies in particular block and destroy their

organism, because these vibrations are **not in line with** the vibrations of beings.

After I no longer felt comfortable in my skin due to stinging and itchy, very unpleasant skin pain, I went to look for the causes. I perceived that LED light is a high-frequency electromagnetic light source.
LED flat-screen televisions are particularly harmful. When buying a screen for a PC, one should also make sure that the screen is not an LED screen. If you switch the PC light to night mode (orange instead of blue light), the negative impact, especially on the eyes, is smaller. Smartphones and the like can also be switched to night mode.
Although LED lights and LED light bulbs have a very long service life, I had to remove these high-frequency light sources from my living spaces and replace them with halogen light.

Electromagnetic current waves, which often flow in an unfiltered state (because there are not enough filter systems) and at a high frequency through all lines in many houses, apartments and workplaces, are an ever-increasing burden for people (for all beings). Unfortunately, the household electricity, which would not have a negative impact on many people in a **filtered** state, is often polluted with high-frequency industrial electricity and more and more often with digital radio microwaves. Electricity and gas are energies that can be fatal in direct contact. Only a mindful and **resource-saving** use of electricity and the increased generation of electricity from solar energy can prevent nuclear power from being generated or imported.
Blocking and destructive **energies, vibrations and emotions** from manipulated (fear-inducing) representations in news and historical traditions, in advertisements, (feature) films, newspapers, magazines, books, stage performances etc. (that serve someone's own purposes and are built on illusions and often cruel delusions) also have a negative impact on beings and their living spaces, **especially when they are brought into their living environment with digital devices, such as smartphones and the like, PCs, televisions, radios, etc.**

2.5. Impacts of electromagnetic, digital and multimedia exposure

In 2017 I made my first conscious and painful experience with **electromagnetic** and **digital** (radio) microwaves and permanent **multimedia** exposure. My husband and I were taking care of our grandchildren, when, in the afternoon, I suddenly had no strength left to lift up my granddaughter any more. Immediately afterwards I got chills and flu-like pain in my limbs without symptoms such as a cold or sore throat.

Due to a long period of rainy weather, my husband had switched on several digital devices (smartphone, the Internet, computer, TV) at the same time; these devices were on from early in the morning until after midnight. I strongly perceived the negative impacts of this and hence wanted to disconnect the wireless Internet. My husband, however, was against me doing so and, therefore, I argued with him over and over again. Not only during the day, but also during the night, he left our landline telephone connection, the wireless Internet and his smartphone switched on. In addition, he let the television programme wash over him during the day and often until after midnight. The electric pasture fence beside us also crackled uninterruptedly, although for weeks no animal was kept in this pasture.

The causes of the energy collapse were “invisible” **electromagnetic** and **digital** (radio) microwaves and permanent **multimedia** exposure in my living environment.

I had to cancel the cycling holiday with a cycling group I had planned together with my husband. My husband then took part in this cycling holiday alone. After he had left the house with his smartphone, the first thing I did was to turn off the main power switch for the power supply. Then I ventilated the house for hours from the cellar to the attic. On the same day, after a walk in the woods, I was painless again, except for pain in my right thigh in the bladder meridian. But as soon as I drank water or ate a dish prepared with water, pain, tiredness and cold sensations flared up again. Due to the permanent exposure to electromagnetic and digital (radio) microwaves and to multimedia in the house over a longer period of time, the tap water (water is an energy carrier) was also electromagnetically and digitally charged and contaminated with blocking and destructive energies, vibrations and emotions from media. So I stopped drinking, eating and showering for the next two days. I was thirsty, but never hungry. While I was staying in the forest or resting in bed, I repeatedly directed my **love within myself** towards my body, my mind and my soul, towards all microorganisms living in symbiosis in my body, towards all natural phenomena, towards all elements (water, wood, fire, earth, metal/air), towards all beings (humans, animals, plants, organisms ...), towards all places (environment, living space) of my being and living as well as towards all relationships, situations and communication within myself, as well as between myself and **all beings and life itself**. On the third day in the morning, I did not feel the pain on my right thigh any more. I therefore assumed that also the tap water had **self-regenerated** again. Completely painless, back in the biorhythmic ecological balance, I was able to drink our water and eat the food prepared with this water again. Being active during the day and deep relaxation during the night in deep sleep were also possible again. I left the power supply switched off all week. Thus, all digital devices in the house were deactivated.

After this event, we took **exposure-reducing measures** in the house. The landline telephone we no longer use is generally unplugged at our home. My husband has deactivated the Internet mode on his smartphone; he only switches it on during the day when he is using it and turns it off during the night. When switched off, he always places it between two pillows filled with sheep's wool. He now gets Internet access again via an Internet landline and he only connects the Internet when he is using it, otherwise the Internet is unplugged.

An electrician has installed a mains disconnection switch in the junction box, with which we can **disconnect** all areas in the house, except the power supply for the heating (power for the circulation pump in winter), the solar collectors and, in the same circuit, a refrigerator. During the night's rest in summer, the electricity supply in our house is completely deactivated. With this mindful and resource-saving approach, we were able to reduce the **electromagnetic**, digital and multimedia exposure level in our house. Our electricity consumption is now much lower than in previous years. For this reason, in the first year after the installation of the mains disconnection switch, we were reimbursed a considerable amount of the electricity prepayments.

Nevertheless, half a year later I had another energetic breakdown because I could no longer protect myself after a series of stresses. In the penultimate week of December, my husband was busy digitizing music cassettes on CDs until the middle of the week. The next day we went on a ski hiking tour on the Handalm (Koralpe) with a very nice hiking colleague of my husband. We also hiked through the wind turbine park. The wind turbines with their many digital devices (remote controls) pollute the wind turbine environment with electromagnetic and digital radiation. Nevertheless, we experienced a sensationally beautiful ski hiking tour, without strong winds and with wonderful snow conditions and pure sunshine. On the way home, our hiking colleague repeatedly used his smartphone for controlling his hearing aid. Due to the smartphone radiation in the car, I got nauseous and dizzy while returning home. After a strong drop in energy in the evening, I got the joint pain I was already familiar with and fever. Hence, I went to bed very early. After my husband had switched on the television set, I could no longer protect myself in this state from the digital satellite radio waves brought into the house. I lay in bed squirming with pain while digital radio microwaves shot through my body like fine pain arrows. Even when my husband turned off the television set, this horror did not stop. Only the deactivation of the electricity supply brought relief after hours. The satellite dish was removed from the roof and my husband now also gets the television programme via the Internet modem.

During the 2018 Football World Cup, many mobile phone operators simultaneously increased the mobile phone radio wave level from 3 to 4. Since the TV and satellite radiation was much higher at the time because of the Football World Cup, many people, including myself, reacted to the suddenly much stronger frequencies with painful body symptoms and immunodeficiency. It cannot have been a coincidence that almost all of my clients and many people in my living environment reacted with various disease symptoms (were ill) during the Football World Cup after the radio wave level 4 had been activated.

Since in autumn 2018 in nearly all municipalities (also in ours) the underground cables were replaced with fibre optic cables and my husband installed a new Internet modem from the Internet provider for a better picture quality at the television set, I felt the digital radio microwaves in a much higher frequency than with the old modem when the modem was activated for the Internet or for the television set. Although the power supply was deactivated during the night's rest, I still noticed high-frequency electromagnetic LED light from the television and high-frequency digital (radio) microwaves in our house in the morning. The high frequencies did no longer dissolve during the night's rest. Since I did not feel comfortable in the house any more, I spent a lot of time in the forest and on the alp in an alpine house, without digital devices in the house. In the forest, on the alp and with daily meridian stretching exercises I was able to reduce the contamination accumulated in the house again and again.

On 4 February 2019, five months after the commissioning of the "new modem", I had a total energetic collapse in my house at night due to "invisible" high-frequency **electromagnetic** and digital (radio) microwaves and multimedia exposure with unbearably burning pain in the middle of my head. A strong wave with high-frequency **electromagnetic and digital** (radio) microwaves destroyed my crown chakra with the flame of life. I had the feeling that my head was torn open in the middle and that through this wound opening high-frequency **electromagnetic and digital** (radio) microwaves, radioactive radiation and metal pollution ... were penetrating the inside of my body. My organism reacted to these suddenly strong and destructive foreign energies, vibrations and emotions with an extreme loss of energy, almost unbearable joint, muscle and bone pain and a severe 3-day diarrhoea with nausea, dizziness, cardiovascular problems and shortness of breath. On the next day, in the morning, my husband took me to the alpine hut, which is free of digital devices. Because of the severe nausea I was only able to drink water after three days, which I then consumed day and night in large quantities. My organism rejected food and even herbal teas (everything from the outside). Although I felt sick, after a few days I tried to eat soup and stewed apples. Since I continued to feel extremely bad, I went to see a doctor who is a yoga colleague of my husband. This doctor was distraught over my condition and had a blood analysis done. The blood analysis indicated a vitamin D3 and B12 deficiency, an impaired iron absorption and a disturbed thyroid function. The inflammation levels in the blood were also extremely high. My urine and stool samples were fine, though. Since I did not tolerate the conventional medications, I filled the mineral depots for D3 and B12 in high doses with

biochemically produced, vegan, gluten- and sugar-free food supplements. I was also allergic to the antibiotic prescribed by my doctor. For this reason, I took 15 drops of grapefruit seed extract (a natural antibiotic) three times a day for one week. In addition, I applied the 5% Lugol's solution, consisting of iodine and potassium iodide, to a thigh in the morning. To detoxify the organism, I took 1 teaspoon of environmentally certified, highly iodine-containing brown algae powder, which even releases radioactive radiation from the body via the stool without damage and provides the organism with many vital and mineral substances. In addition, I drank a lot of clean and pure water with a good pH value.

In the beginning I could only reactivate my energy flows with meditation. After one week it was possible for me to do my meridian stretching exercises with five breaths. Gradually, I was able to increase the exercises again to 20 breaths. Due to **electromagnetic**, digital and chemical (metal) pollution in the organism, I became an even **stronger antenna** for electromagnetic and digital (radio) microwaves.

Hence, during my regeneration, we made sure that the power was almost always switched off in the house with the mains disconnection switch and that digital devices such as the Internet, the smartphone and the television were deactivated (completely switched off) in the house. A smartphone switched to airplane mode does nothing to protect against digital radio microwaves. Only after many weeks of patience and training, many meditations and a seasonally adapted diet that is in line with the seasonal biorhythm, with lots of wild garlic, ground ivy, stinging nettles and dandelion (spring herbs), was my energy balance restored. From this time on it was possible for me to hike in the protection of the forests again.

So I stayed on the alp for a weekend while my husband stayed at home. Because I was not in the house during these two days, he activated the Internet and the television set very often in the house. He still could not quite believe that the causes of my symptoms were electromagnetic and digital (radio) microwaves ..., but still hoped that the causes of the symptoms could be other health problems.

Already in the first night at home my organism reacted to the electromagnetic, digital and multimedia exposure in the house at night with the same symptoms as on 4 February. This time I did not wait until morning, but asked my husband to take me to the alp immediately, although it was only 1:30 o'clock am. Since

I left the **contaminated environment** immediately after I had noticed the symptoms, the wound on my head and almost all symptoms healed within a week.
The cause of the last two energy collapses in 2019 was the newly installed modem for Internet access in our house. A SIM card was installed in the modem, which brought the Internet into the house at the highest frequency available (probably already 5G). Since distributors in shorter distances are needed for 5G, I also assume that a WLAN distributor function was installed in the modem and that we provided a "transmission mast" in the house at that time, unintentionally and without being informed. Such WLAN distributors are also installed at the power distributors, which is why the power is also contaminated with digital radio microwaves. This possible modem radiation load in the house was also pointed out to us by a very far-sighted doctor, who stood by me with medical help at that time. After researching the modem, it was immediately removed by my husband. Although the old modem transmits at lower frequencies, due to my now even more sensitive body reactions, we have to be very careful with all digital devices and always deactivate them when not in use when I am in the house. **(This should actually be a matter of course in every home and in the environment of other living beings when using such media with care, as with smoking.)** Many uninformed mobile phone and Internet users do not know that they could **switch off high frequencies** (e.g. prevent 5G), because this possibility is not brought to our attention.

I perceive **electromagnetic** and **digital** (radio) waves as (high-frequency) **microwaves**, which block, and in very bad cases paralyse, the free energy circulation, the chakras and the acupuncture points, preferably in the brain, in the central channel (spine) and in the heart centre.
You can only protect yourself against **electromagnetic** and digital (radio) microwaves from radio masts, satellites, fibre-optic cables, telephone and power lines, horizontal contamination and against multimedia pollution **brought into your living environment (house, car, etc.)** if you deactivate digital devices or remove them from your living environment, switch off the power supply, do not use LED light, destroy all barcodes and live media-free.
I can well imagine that smartphones and the like with activated Internet access even transfer fingerprints, which are then stored for the identification of

people. Nowadays, humans are also offered electronic chips (similar to cattle), which are implanted under the skin, for the identification data ("glass monitoring"). It seems that in the case of some parcel delivery companies, you can now only sign with your finger on the smartphone when accepting a parcel.

You can protect yourself from **electromagnetic**, often high-frequency current waves with digital radio microwaves due to WLAN distributors and from unnecessary financial burdens with a mains disconnection switch installed in the junction box, with which you can **disconnect the power supply** in all areas (rooms) of the house where no electricity is needed.
I recommend the following **first measures** to people who react to electromagnetic current waves, digital radio microwaves, magnetism ... and to multimedia exposure with symptoms: disconnect the power supply to the Internet, the landline telephone, PCs, televisions, radios and electrical appliances when not in use by unplugging them or generally switch off the electricity supply when not in use, de-energise at least all sleeping areas in the junction box, remove SIM cards from mobile phones, destroy all barcodes, **remove** membership cards, cashpoint cards and the like, battery-powered devices (including electronic children's toys) **from the living spaces**, avoid multimedia exposure and screen radiation (especially with LED light), remove unused things, also newspapers, magazines, books, etc., from the living environment and only use halogen light sources.

If one is in a process of detoxification, purification and clear-out of the body, mind and soul, one would also like to **clear out** the living space with house, yard and garden and all relationships, situations and communication within oneself, as well as between oneself and all beings and life itself, in singledom and coupledom, as well as in professional, business, leisure and social life.
We had the asphalt removed from our driveway and the entrance to the house paved with natural stones. The house built 40 years ago with bricks (38 cm diameter) was cleared out from the cellar to the attic. We have also removed books and magazines with blocking and destructive energies, vibrations and emotions from all living spaces. We cook our food on a wood-fired kitchen stove only. We no longer use electrical appliances when preparing our food. With this way of life, we live more healthily and more independently of

electricity. Gradually we will replace contaminated floors, furnishings, etc. with untreated natural solid wood.
In a metal-free, natural organic solid wood bed, on an organic mattress made of natural materials, with pillow, blanket and mattress topper made of organic cotton and filled with organic sheep's wool and in a generally currentless, clean and healthy room climate, without electromagnetic, digital and multimedia influences from TV, mobile phone, the Internet, etc., I can almost always regenerate and recover in the night biorhythm in deep sleep.
Today I would only have a heat-insulating and radiation-proof natural solid wood house built from 100% moon wood, also because **this building material is ecological and sustainable**. In rooms where no electricity is needed, I would never have electrical wiring laid again.

I distance myself from examinations and treatments with electromagnetically powered devices, except in genuine emergencies or after accidents, because in such examinations and treatments one is confronted with electromagnetic and digital (radio) microwaves and media exposure. In bioresonance examinations and treatments, which are performed with electromagnetically powered devices, one is also confronted with such energies, vibrations and emotions. As soon as you have placed your hands on the copper plate (copper attracts energies extremely fast and passes them on extremely fast), you will be exposed not only to electromagnetic and digital pollution, but also to "intolerances and diseases" programmed in the device, such as viral energies, Lyme disease and other bacterial energies, pathogens, etc. If one goes into resonance with such energies, vibrations and emotions, then already existing symptoms will become even stronger, or even new symptoms could occur. Furthermore, the central nervous system could react extremely after such examinations or treatments.
Since two doctors have dealt with "electrosensitivity" from a medical point of view and published a book with the title "ELEKTROSENSIBEL – Strahlenflüchtlinge in einer Funkvernetzten Gesellschaft" (ELECTROSENSITIVE – radiation refugees in a radio-networked society), orthodox medicine has also considered the ever-increasing chemical, electromagnetic and digital environmental pollution as a possible cause of the symptoms of its patients.

2.6. A mindful use of electricity can protect you against digital pollution

Due to the media situation, I have been distancing myself from multimedia channels, such as TV, radio and newspapers, for 13 years now.
I handle electricity and digital devices very carefully and with gratitude. I only switch on my key phone without Internet access once a day. I communicate almost exclusively via SMS and only in exceptional cases with the hands-free system.
I only visit cultural events (concerts, performances) with good vibrations. A cousin of mine took part in a musical for self-discovery and peace on our earth. I was very thrilled and deeply touched by this performance, in which many children enjoyed living out their musical talents. I had a similar experience when I was at a concert of a Swedish vocal group. The group community with three male and two female voices was perfectly in harmony and balance. At a New Year's concert in my husband's home municipality with a string orchestra, which I visit enthusiastically every year with my husband, I almost always feel comfortable, too.
Before I visit public events, I direct my love towards all beings present at the event venue and towards my self-protection. By means of telepathy I send my request to the visitors and organisers that they leave their mobile phones at home or in the car and, if they take smartphones or the like to the event, that they switch them off during the event or only switch them on when they use them.
When hiking, cycling, skiing or travelling within a group, I ask the group members to deactivate digital devices (smartphones and the like, sports watches, GPS units, cameras, odometers, etc.) during my presence and to switch them on only when they use them or, if it is possible, to completely dispense with digital devices. Out of **self-protection**, I avoid an environment in which this attentiveness is not (yet) possible, also because it is very arduous to constantly have to justify oneself.
Due to their body reactions, often with strong and unpleasant pain, people with highly sensitive perceptions are prepared to take measures to reduce electrical pollution and to handle media such as smartphones and the like, the Internet, PCs, televisions, etc. with care. People lacking conscious perception

often have no motivation and no understanding for a "limited" use of these media in the environment of highly sensitive people.
All natural phenomena (including human beings), however, are affected by this—probably the greatest—environmental pollution.

For many people, reading a daily newspaper at breakfast is part of their breakfast ritual. When my husband reads the daily newspaper during breakfast, I avoid to get close to him because he is almost always negative and above all extremely sensitive to noise. Since he is otherwise a very attentive, nice and sociable person, I assume that the cause of this negative mood is not his nature, but blocking and destructive energies, vibrations and emotions from the sensationalist and often manipulated news from the daily newspaper, with which he goes into resonance while reading.
For this reason, when my husband fetches the newspaper in the morning, I always imagine that the newspaper reporters, **uninfluencedly**, only disseminate true, wise and knowledge-based information from power sources of light and love. If many readers of my book imagine it this way, then it will surely be the case at some point, because energies follow our expectations.

There are people who like to solve Sudokus and crosswords in daily newspapers, preferably in the morning during breakfast. These people take their breakfast without giving it a single thought, without enjoying it and often also without being grateful for it. Immediately after getting up, these people, most of whom are overly intellectual, activate and train their head brain (which is dominant anyway). Although this training keeps them rationally and mentally fit, their intuition and instincts (their belly brain) are more and more pushed into the background. As a result, their intuition, instincts and common sense can be thrown out of balance.

2.7. Other examples of electromagnetic, digital and multimedia exposure

Many years ago, after eating a vegetable strudel reheated in a microwave in a restaurant, I already felt the high-frequency electromagnetic microwaves,

especially in my head (brain) and back (spinal cord), so uncomfortably that, even then, I had to go to bed for hours with unpleasant pain, after a sharp drop in my energy levels.
A telescopic prosthesis with various metals on the upper jaw nearly became my downfall due to increasing electromagnetic and digital stress. The metals of the prosthesis attracted electromagnetic and digital (radio) microwaves. High levels of pollution blocked my energy flows in the jaw and head area. The consequences were not only a drop in my energy levels, but also severe pain in the head and ear area, cardiovascular problems and sleep disorders. Before I fortunately found a very competent dentist who removed this trouble spot in my mouth with a metal-free all-ceramic solution, I could sleep neither during the day nor at night.

A client who runs a large company told me that there was a lot of unrest in the company's offices. Office workers feel overwhelmed by their work and many employees are demotivated. A very good employee, who, due to the management of the company's vehicle fleet, uses smartphones (often one on each ear) to make calls from morning to evening, jumps into the fresh air again and again, and then only makes phone calls outdoors, because he is often no longer able to sit quietly in the office. My client, the managing director of the company, also time and again has the feeling that she can no longer do the work in the company in a rhythmic workflow. Electromagnetic, digital and multimedia exposure due to digital devices and LED light sources in offices are certainly also a cause of feeling overwhelmed at work, stress situations and subsequently burnout that should not be underestimated.
The managing director is now considering leaving the office once a day for half an hour together with the office staff and exercising together in the fresh air, so that the employees can get rid of the electromagnetic, digital and multimedia contamination accumulated. During the recovery break, she will ensure that digital devices such as PCs and smartphones are turned off, the Internet is disabled and all offices are well ventilated. In a good room climate and feeling recuperated, the employees will certainly be motivated again and will be able to continue working creatively.

When the magnetic field mats were booming, a friend of mine lay down on a **magnetic** field mat and was additionally irradiated with light effects. Since her organism was unable to cope with so many external influences, she had an epileptic seizure, even though she had never had one in her life.

10 years ago, a strong boom was seen in atlas correction, which was offered by people not trained in orthodox medicine with a new electronic device on the market. Electromagnetic waves were supplied to people in such treatments via the atlas, which is energetically responsible for self-control, self-guidance and a "strong spine", directly through the central channel. Even at the very idea of what was done to these people, I still get chills today. Meanwhile such treatments are forbidden. Electronic massage devices, which are also offered for sale as shiatsu massage devices, should also be absolutely avoided, since **electromagnetic** waves, which are not in line with the vibration of people, will block the free flow of energy **even more**.

A young mother came to me with her 3-month-old and fully breastfed baby. Until the third month her baby was calm and equable during the day and at night it already had sleep phases of up to six hours. Because the baby cried day and night after the third month and was very restless, the child was diagnosed as a "bawler" by orthodox medicine. Lately, time and again, the older son of the family also has had attacks of aggression during the day and nightmares with anxiety attacks at night.
The parents of the children did not know that microwave ovens and induction cookers as well as induction dishes with a magnetic core contaminate the food and living environment with high-frequency **electromagnetic** waves and that activated digital devices such as the Internet, smartphones, PCs, televisions and monitors have a negative effect on the well-being of their children. The parents are now very careful with electricity, digital devices (smartphones, the Internet, television, PCs ...) and multimedia pollution in the house. Shortly after they started to protect their children's living and sleeping areas from such pollution, the baby stopped crying in a **disturbance-free environment**. The sleep phases at night became longer and longer and after a short time, the girl slept through the nights. Her brother's nightmares with anxiety attacks and his attacks of aggression also improved significantly.

If living areas, especially the sleeping areas, are free of electromagnetic, digital and multimedia pollution brought into the house, if the rooms are equipped with good biological and ecological natural materials and are always well ventilated, then children and adults will feel comfortable in a clean and healthy room climate. Blankets, pillows and mattress toppers made of organic cotton and filled with organic sheep's wool protect against digital and electromagnetic pollution during the night. Ecological and biological food and clothing as well as body, laundry and home care are equally important for the development of children in the biorhythmic ecological balance and in a comprehensively healthy growth.

Parents who do not live identically to the love residing within themselves in their **identity- and individuality-based behaviour** often follow given trends out of group pressure and due to their strong outward orientation. With this behaviour they also take a toll on their offspring: with high-tech shoes which have irregular light effects, with electronic toys made of materials that are harmful to health and that bring children out of ecological balance, as well as with non-biological and often uncomfortable clothes made of bad materials (on which idols from the multimedia world are depicted, who are emulated diligently by the offspring).

Synthetic fibres, metal glitter effects and magnetic fasteners on clothing become electromagnetically charged and attract digital (radio) microwaves, which then block the energy flows, chakras and acupuncture points and weaken the immune system.

Conventional cleaning agents used in household and laundry care, such as harmful household cleaners, washing powder and fabric softeners with fragrances, cannot be biologically degraded and pollute not only the environment, but above all human beings and especially children. When people wear clothes "contaminated" with washing powder and fabric softener and are confronted with such laundry while sleeping, this often has a significant impact on their health. The same goes for non-organic body care, because harmful substances get into the blood via the skin. Denatured, non-organic food with many sweets, which parents and grandparents often eat themselves, can be the cause of restlessness, concentration disorders, attacks of aggression, anxiety and sleep disorders.

Parents and their children who live out (self-)blocking and (self-)destructive social, sexual, nature-specific, lifestyle-related, dietary, consumer and decision-making behaviours that are caused by an imbalance of "giving and taking" are often ill because their immune system is weakened over and over again by such behaviours.

2.8. Laundry, clothing, household and body care

As already described in the previous chapter, clothing made of synthetic fibres and glitter effects (also on natural materials) become electromagnetically and digitally charged. Many people are electromagnetically and digitally charged to an extreme degree—both by their clothes (often made from bad [artificial] materials) and by their environment (carpet and plastic floors, carpets, electric current which flows unnecessarily through all lines and many activated digital devices); this blocks the **energy flows with their own dynamic energy supply**. Environmental organisations have repeatedly found in studies that clothing, including baby and children's clothing, is heavily contaminated with chemicals and plasticisers. When buying linen and clothing, if you do not want to expose yourself and your family to harmful substances, you have to make sure that they are made from a natural organic material, tested for harmful substances and fairly traded.
Clothing made of organic materials is often offered as "tested for harmful substances" in supermarkets at very low prices. After the purchase of such low-price offers I noticed that clothing and linen (bed linen, etc.) are heavily contaminated with plasticisers up to the **upper limit values** for harmful substances. Plasticisers and fabric softeners in clothing and linen **weaken people's identity- and individuality-based behaviour**. In addition, the chemical substances in plasticisers are harmful to health. When I buy new clothes or linen, I always wash the clothes or linen at the highest possible temperature with 1 tablespoon of sodium carbonate (washing soda) and 1 tablespoon of sodium bicarbonate (baking soda). Sodium carbonate and sodium bicarbonate (dissolves acids and odours) clean the laundry of chemical substances.

Babies and children can be protected from skin irritation and soreness by abstaining from contaminated wet wipes and toilet paper and by washing the baby's bottom with warm water under the water pipe after defecation instead or by cleaning the bottom with an organic flannel moistened with warm water. My own children and my grandchildren were always very enthusiastic about these cleansing rituals. I also use an organic flannel moistened with warm water instead of toilet paper for cleaning after defecation. Instead of using paper handkerchiefs contaminated with harmful substances, I (again) use organic linen handkerchiefs.

I primarily use hot water for cleaning and washing dishes. I only use the dishwasher when I have guests. The dishes from the dishwasher washed with ½ tablespoon of sodium carbonate and ½ tablespoon of sodium bicarbonate are always very clean and odourless. For stubborn dirt in the household, I use cleaning lime. When my granddaughter recently wrote on the kitchen table with a ballpoint pen in her flow of creativity, I was even able to remove ballpoint pen stains effortlessly with cleaning lime. Washbasins, pots, pans, stoves, etc. always look like new when cleaned with cleaning lime powder.

Heavily burnt pots can be cleaned very well with sodium carbonate by leaving some sodium carbonate with hot water in the pot for one hour. Sodium carbonate and sodium bicarbonate are the best universal cleaners for me; **they have a "basic" effect on the drainage system and do not pollute the environment.** In the evening I put sodium carbonate powder, sodium bicarbonate and some hot water in dirty drains and toilets. Even urine scale can be removed with this application. I clean clogged drains the next day with a force cup and lots of water. My laundry washed with 1 tablespoon of sodium carbonate and 1 tablespoon of sodium bicarbonate at the highest possible temperature is always very clean, odourless and feels neither too soft nor too rough.

For more than 10 years I have not used any cosmetics (no shower gel, no face and body creams, etc.), because harmful substances also get into the blood via the skin. Instead, I rub my face and body with a rough towel in the morning or in the evening, lovingly but vigorously. Once a week, mostly in the course of hair washing, I do a full body peeling with a regional, untreated, organic fine-grained natural salt from my kitchen. After rubbing or the salt peeling my skin feels soft and well supplied with blood. Before these applications my skin often itched and I often did not feel well "in my skin". Since I have been doing this active and almost free body care, none of these symptoms occur any more. During skin rubbing and the salt peeling, dead body cells are removed from the

skin, the lymph and the meridians (energy pathways) are activated and the **immune system is strengthened**. Not only the skin, but the entire organism (body), the mind and the soul regenerate after these applications from their own dynamic power.
For my physical and mental fitness, I have been doing meridian stretching and muscle strengthening exercises every day in the morning for the last 10 years. Once a week I enjoy gymnastics within a gymnastics group.

A very effective and simple muscle-building exercise is when you sit on the floor or on a chair, lean your upper arms against your body and support your elbows at your hips, tighten your biceps with a firm fist, slowly bring your forearms up with 10 breaths and slowly bring them down again with 10 breaths. The exercise should be repeated at least five times and the biceps tension must always be maintained during the exercises. All muscles in the organism receive muscle **growth** impulses from the biceps of the upper arms and by imagining muscle growth.

2.8.1. Healing and purifying effects of organic coconut oil

For my neighbour, who suffers from neurodermatitis and had an open finger for half a year, I made a comfrey healing ointment with extra virgin organic coconut oil. I heated the finely chopped herbs in the organic coconut oil in a cooking pot; **shortly before the boiling point was reached**, I took the herb-oil mixture from the stove, poured it into a glass bowl and left it covered overnight. In the morning I strained the oil. I filled the liquid herbal healing ointment, which solidified during cooling, into screw cap jars. After a few applications the finger of my neighbour was healed.
One of my husband's fingers was heavily swollen due to an injury with a splinter of wood and inflamed with a suppurative focus. After the second application with the same healing ointment the inflammation with the suppurative focus was healed. Based on these experiences I became aware of the antibacterial properties of coconut oil. Since then I have been using the extra virgin, fairly traded organic coconut oil from sun-drenched coconuts, which have been **organically grown** by Filipino smallholders, as a non-regional

exception not only for the production of organic healing ointments, but also for oral hygiene, for my hair, in winter once a week for the supply of solar energy (vitamin D) via the skin and in the household.

Since coconut oil contains a large proportion of saturated fatty acid, I use it very sparingly in my diet and prefer it for the following **external applications**:

Oral hygiene: Teeth brushed with organic coconut oil are very clean and the coconut oil has an antibacterial effect in the mouth.
Oil pulling: Immediately after getting up, push 1 tablespoon of organic coconut oil back and forth in the mouth for 10 minutes. Since the oil-saliva mixture contains many bacteria and toxins, separately dispose of the oil-saliva mixture as a harmful substance. Oil pulling reduces harmful plaque and thus the risk of tooth decay. It counteracts inflammation and periodontosis (shrinking gums).
Important note: If your teeth have metal fillings (amalgam, etc.), do not pull oil under any circumstances, as heavy metals could be washed out by oil pulling.

Hair and skin care: Coconut oil has a caring and regulating effect on the scalp, hair roots and hair. It nourishes stressed hair, helps with hair loss and split ends. Let some coconut oil melt in your hands and knead it lightly into dry hair with your hands.
If the scalp is dry and in case of dandruff or itching, massage the coconut oil into the scalp. Put your hair up, wrap your head in a towel and let it work in overnight. Wash your hair in the morning with a mild biological hair soap.
Thanks to its antimicrobial properties, coconut oil fights bacterial skin infections and skin fungi. It also helps with acne and blackheads.
Wash your face with warm water, massage 1 teaspoon of coconut oil into your skin, wet a small towel with hot water and place it on your face until the towel is cold. Repeat this procedure two to three times. Coconut oil can also be used for stretch marks, neurodermatitis and nosebleeds (apply the oil to the inside of the nostrils).
Instead of deodorants, which could clog the sweat glands and contain harmful substances, one should use a mixture of organic coconut oil and lavender. Heat lavender flowers in a cooking pot with organic coconut oil which contains up to 60% of antibacterial lauric acid; **shortly before the boiling point is reached**, remove the mixture from the stove, pour it into a glass bowl and leave it

covered overnight. The next day strain the oil, fill it into small screw cap jars and store it in a cool place.

Insect and tick protection: Massage extra virgin organic coconut oil into the skin (hands, feet, neck, naked skin). The protection is even stronger if you use a homemade mixture of organic coconut oil and lavender or organic coconut oil and nut. The organic coconut oil-nut ointment, which is made from green walnuts, is also suitable for rubbing the abdomen in case of flatulence. The organic coconut oil-lavender ointment could also be used against fungal infections (athlete's foot).

Household care: Oil wooden cutting boards regularly with coconut oil. Rub the coconut oil well into the dry board, let the oil seep in overnight and rub off the excess oil in the morning. The wood does not become brittle and bacteria have no chance due to the lauric acid. Bronze can also be cleaned and polished with coconut oil and a cotton cloth. With a dash of lemon juice you have the perfect wood polish.
Lubricate rusty utensils with a thin layer of oil, leave it on for 1 hour and then rinse it off.

Important information: Please do not confuse the extra virgin, fairly traded organic coconut oil produced by small organic farmers with the conventionally grown palm oil, for which the rainforest is being cut down and pushed back even more due to the strong demand for palm oil and its versatile use. With this non-organic and non-ecological approach, the biorhythmic ecological balance on our planet is even more destroyed. In addition, more and more profitable palm trees are being grown on existing arable land instead of food for the population.
In 2017, an environmental organisation tested palm oil-containing branded products in the **food trade**. In many (branded) products, high concentrations of harmful, probably carcinogenic and mutagenic substances have been found, which could be particularly dangerous for children. During the production of refined palm oil harmful substances are produced because the oil is heated to a high temperature so that it is neutral in taste and odour. Cold-pressed organic palm oil without health-endangering bleaching substances can be recognised by its orange colouring.

Never heat virgin (cold-pressed) oils, as harmful substances may be produced during heating and valuable vitamins may be lost. Only add cold-pressed oils to food after cooking. For heating there are special heat-resistant oils.

2.9. People need space and order to develop their creativity

Free yourself in your living and working environment from things that are not needed (any more) (from the "junk of everyday life"), such as newspapers, magazines, books, jewellery, home accessories and gifts that only stress you and occupy space ... People need space and order to develop their creativity, talents and vocations. There are people who live in great confinement, in a "warehouse for old, collected and no longer used things", without space and order for themselves and their families. These people pay the rent or the acquisition and operating costs for their house/flat primarily not for themselves to live and to develop their creativity, talents and vocations in a feel-good housing environment with space and order, but for things they have collected in their coercive behaviour and things usually not needed (any more), from which they cannot separate. For many of these people, their own flat or house is only a place to spend the night, because they flee as often as possible from their flat or house due to extreme (self-)confinement with little space for all family members. In such living situations it happens again and again that family members find their "living room" outside of their own home—in restaurants, coffee houses ... or with friends.

3.1. (Self-)destruction has serious consequences

The causes of (self-)destruction of the physical, mental and spiritual well-being in soul, family and world peace (peace in the world, in worlds and between worlds), in the biorhythmic ecological balance, in peace and in harmony within oneself, as well as between oneself and all beings and life itself, in a comprehensively healthy growth and in the flow of being and living, where, in all energy flows, **exclusively love flows freely in a closed cycle**, within oneself, as well as between oneself and natural phenomena, elements (water, wood, fire, earth, metal/air) and beings (humans, animals, plants, organisms ..., microorganisms living in symbiosis in beings and macroorganisms living in symbiosis with beings), **within oneself, as well as between oneself and beings and life itself**, are (self-)blocking and (self-)destructive manifestations, fixations or fanaticisms built on illusions, delusions and hallucinations (that go deep into people's patterns of thought and belief and entail not only (self-)blocking and (self-)destructive social, sexual, nature-specific, lifestyle-related, dietary, consumer and decision-making behaviours involving an imbalance of "giving and taking", but also abuses of confidence, disregard for boundaries, competence withdrawals, deprivations of the right of decision-making, paternalism and infantilising, physical, mental, spiritual, elemental and environmental contamination and injuries, resource exploitations, etc.) in being and living, in cycles of being and living, in places (environment, living spaces ...) of being and living, in relationships, situations and communication within oneself, as well as between oneself and beings and life itself, in singledom and coupledom, as well as in professional, business, leisure and social life. The worst consequences are (religious) wars, as the past has shown us again and again.

The 30-year war and forced Christianisations on almost all continents of the world were consequences of a (self-)destructive religious fanaticism in Christianity. At present, religious wars are responsible for the fact that many people are fleeing their homeland.

During World War II and the National Socialist era, fanatical social classifications as well as fanatical being- and gender-specific evaluations built on illusions, delusions and hallucinations (that went deep into people's patterns of thought and belief) were the cause of traumatic and terrible events. Power obsession and imperiousness were the causes why Jews (a race rejected by the leader) were driven out of the country or killed. People, including mentally and physically handicapped people, were gassed or fell victim, together with animals, to boundary-disregarding experiments in medicine, research, racial breeding, etc.

Unfortunately, many people did not see through this system at that time; instead, falling victim to a mass hysteria, they went into resonance with the manipulations and deceptions, illusions and delusions of National Socialism, which was spread multimedially, and for the leader's own purposes, in many

announcements and via news, by the leader himself or by manipulated, remote-controlled and misprogrammed vicarious agents of the power system. Although many people today are still traumatised by these terrible events of the past, still not all people distance themselves from such systems. People often follow blindly, without forming their own opinions, (power) people, leaders, idols ... from systems with (self-)destructive fanaticism, for which they become vicarious agents who are stuck in roles of victim and perpetrator.
Power, money and/or fear-inducing representations use such systems specifically for their purposes. News agencies often also become—consciously or unconsciously—vicarious agents in **representations of information**.
In the multimedia world (i.e. the Internet, TV, radio, newspapers, magazines, books, announcements, films, stage representations, etc.), manipulated representations of such systems serving someone's own purposes are disseminated again and again, especially in advertisements, news and historical traditions.
Representations serving someone's own purposes, spread over the Internet, reach many people in a fast and targeted manner. This marketing opportunity is not only used by retailers, the industry and many companies for their products, but also by many politicians and evaluation-oriented systems for the formation of the desired mass opinions, moods and hysterias among the people.
You can **only protect** yourself from manipulations and deceptions from representations serving someone's own purposes and embodying blocking and destructive theories, views and opinions from external influences (multimedially from the Internet, TV, radio, newspapers, magazines, books, films, announcements, stage representations, etc.) and from manipulated, remote-controlled mass opinions, moods and hysterias if you **distance and dissociate** yourself from manipulated multimedia influences from the outer world.
Although, also because of the media situation, I have been distancing and dissociating myself from media such as the Internet, TV, radio, newspapers, magazines, books, films, announcements, stage representations, etc. with manipulations, deceptions and blocking and destructive energies, vibrations and emotions for 13 years, information that is important for me always comes to me. I draw the pure, clear, all-encompassing and perfect, unadulterated truth and wisdom, the pure, clear and all-encompassing knowledge, without

consuming any resources and with all-embracing gratitude, from the **power source of light and love residing within myself**.

3.2. Airborne pollution

There are almost no more people who do not worry about the condensation trails of airplanes that pollute the often sunny and cloudless horizon. Sensitive beings (humans, animals, plants, organisms ...) react to chemical substances, radioactive radiation, magnetism, electromagnetic and digital radio microwaves with painful physical symptoms, but also with fear and nightmares with anxiety attacks.
My youngest daughter did research on the Internet and found a publication. It says that chemical substances, which do not occur on our earth in such a way, were found in water samples in different places throughout Germany. It is therefore assumed that theories such as "chemical air attack" could be true. Unfortunately, to this day, no environmental organisation or politician has taken a stand on this issue and informed people about this phenomenon.
Since 2017, water communities (including ours) have been confronted with "germs in the water" after inspections. For this reason, the drinking water must be chemically treated. Sensitive people like me react to chemically treated, acidic tap water with nausea and diarrhoea. I have tested the pH value of tap water in my immediate surroundings.
Even the water on the alp had a poor pH value, although this water is not confronted with any chemical pollution from agriculture or the industry.
For 40 years I have drunk our drinking water, obtained from an alp, directly from the water pipe. Since 2017 I can only drink tap water in a boiled state.
Although I was still very proud of our clean rivers in 2016, I have not been able to bathe in them since the summer of 2017 due to visible accumulations of contamination particles. Fortunately, I could observe that brooks and rivers were optically clean again in spring after the winter.
My explanation for the unstable, rainy weather with often cold temperatures, with which we were confronted in June 2018 and also in the year 2019 since the beginning of May in long-lasting periods, is that the ascending water molecules are also electromagnetically, digitally and radioactively charged and

contaminated with metal particles. For this reason, they can no longer float in the air for a long time. Clean water molecules are light and float freely in a cloud accumulation for a very long time, until the cloud dissolves again sometime **in the biorhythm of the water cycle. Even the sun's rays can often no longer penetrate the contaminated fog.** More and more people are confronted with the fact that they are no longer able to hold their urine in a controlled way. The bladder reacts (similar to an inflammation of the bladder) with incontinence to the contaminated water ingested.

Due to ever-increasing physical, mental, spiritual and environmental contamination and injuries, the self-purifying, self-regenerating, self-transforming and self-healing powers in all natural phenomena, elements, beings (humans, animals, plants, organisms ...), **in all beings and life itself**, have to cope with ever-increasing stresses. When I wanted to detoxify myself in 2019 with medically certified zeolite (volcanic rock powder), my symptoms became even worse. I therefore assume that the volcanic rock powder was also radioactively, electromagnetically, digitally and metallically contaminated.

In recent years, doctors have increasingly been confronted with patients suffering from whooping cough-like coughing fits and diarrhoea.

A homoeopathic doctor got to the bottom of this phenomenon of coughing fits and had her patients' blood examined for whooping cough. Their patients did not suffer from whooping cough, but had to cough out extreme contaminations from the lungs with whooping cough-like coughing fits.

Particularly alternative doctors call on environmental organisations and politicians to take a stand on the "phenomenon in the air".

Pollution of the soil, water and air (the elements) is certainly also caused by non-organically managed industries, strongly profit-oriented conventional agriculture, nurseries, vineyards and orchards, and unfortunately also by many private households due to chemical applications (artificial fertilisers, pesticides, herbicides ...). A problem in conventional agriculture with factory farming is also the liquid manure and the biggest problem of environmental pollution are the "invisible" and often high-frequency electromagnetic and digital (radio) microwaves ....

3.3. Actions to protect the environment

Environmental organisations draw our attention to the destruction of the environment time and again.
In December 2017 I wrote this letter to the mayor of my home municipality due to an environmental protection action of an environmental organisation:
"Dear Mayor,
Recently you received an email from an environmental organisation about the harmful and mutagenic effects of glyphosate in herbicides.
This year at the beginning of August wild bees and bumble bees have suddenly disappeared. They are believed to have died of immunodeficiency due to contact with pesticides and environmental toxins. Hopefully the brood will survive the winter. When I learned from a study that 60% of the pesticides sold are sold to private households, I was shocked. If our municipality, which participates in the "Healthy Municipality" campaign, no longer uses glyphosate in public places as an environmentally conscious model, then many citizens of our municipality would certainly follow this example and perhaps completely do without chemicals in the future, especially in private households."
Municipalities could motivate their citizens to maintain biodiversity through the "healthy municipality" campaign. Then many citizens would certainly become active for the maintenance of biodiversity, would sow flower meadows on part of their land for (wild) bees, bumble bees (nectar-collecting insects), butterflies, etc. and would only mow existing natural meadows with many flowers once the plants are ready to shed their seeds. In order to secure the seed release, the mown grass should dry on the meadow for two days. Grass that has started to dry or dry hay is a wonderful organic material for mulching and composting.
Recently, it said in the newspaper that many convinced farmers as well as wine and fruit growers will voluntarily do without herbicides in the future. The head of a company has also piped up and publicly declared that this company will only buy glyphosate-free food and offer it to customers. This example will be followed by other food companies for reasons of competition.
In the meantime, the Carinthian state government has publicly announced that Carinthia will be the first state in Austria to stop using glyphosate in public

places. Hopefully other states, many countries and above all many farmers, nurseries and many private households will follow this example.

3.4. Entirely profit-driven and conventionally managed farms are destroying the ecological balance

On farms that are only run "for profit", monocultures and rationalisation measures with chemical aids are the causes of pollution and exploitation of fields, meadows, forests and farm animals.
For the feed in factory farming, the soil is increasingly leached with monocultures and polluted with chemicals. In my childhood the maize seeds were always sown at a distance of an adult's foot so that each maize plant had enough space and nutrients for its growth. This distance has long since ceased to be maintained; instead, the maize plants receive a lot of artificial fertiliser for their hybrid growth. They are treated with pesticides against diseases and insect infestation and with herbicides against weeds.
Chemical substances pollute soils, brooks, rivers, lakes and also the drinking water in the long term. The soils of many fields of monocultures are poisoned, leached and compacted to the point that they could only regenerate again in a closed cycle after a break in field cultivation with special green manuring and ecological or organic cultivation.
Green manure plants detoxify the soil, enrich it with nitrogen and revive soil life. Meanwhile, green manure plants are also sown by conventional farmers after harvesting in summer. However, these fields would have to be cultivated in spring without **destroying the soil life**. Unfortunately, many (maize) fields are still being dug over (the earth is turned from bottom to top) before winter. With this approach humans destroy the ecological balance of the soil with the many microorganisms and macroorganisms, because the soil life at the earth's surface **dies by the score without protection**.
Due to liquid manure, artificial fertiliser and the use of pesticides, biodiversity is being lost more and more. In the past, a wide strip of wild meadow was always left between fields and waysides or roadsides. Today one can observe more and more that the fields are dug over up to the wayside or roadside. Apart from dandelion and clover, there are almost no flowers and medicinal

herbs left on the meadows of conventional farmers. Such meadows are overfertilised with liquid manure from factory farming so that the grass can be harvested four times a year, mostly for silage. Plants are not allowed to shed their seeds on the meadows of conventional farmers; this compromises plant diversity.
This phenomenon is also spreading more and more on the land of private households. In many private households, the grass on meadows and lawns is short-cut every week in summer. Caught up in perfectionism, lawn owners even use herbicides to remove unwanted meadow herbs from their lawns or cover the ground with a plastic film that takes the breath away from soil life, so that wild plants no longer grow between cultivated plants.
Unfortunately, house and land owners who are strongly outwardly oriented and probably "uninformed" still resort to herbicides, pesticides and artificial fertilisers because they can no longer see, care for and enjoy the beauty of untouched nature.
With hybrid seeds and hybrid plants, herbicides, pesticides and artificial fertilisers, they often grow their own vegetables and fruit. Especially when they compete with their neighbours in growing fruit and vegetables.

A gymnastics colleague told us that, after using a glyphosate-containing herbicide to remove the grass between the paving stones, her roses, growing at least one metre away, suffered a total slump in growth. Although her roses normally bloom beautifully every year, only a few mutilated flowers appeared after this poison application. After that experience, she will never use any herbicide again.
I hope that soon legal provisions will generally prevent "free access" to pesticides, especially to herbicides, and that medicinal and wild plants will be protected by law on part of the land owned by companies or individuals and especially in public places until they have shed their seeds.
Fortunately, there are more and more people who have realised that when one natural phenomenon is lost, all other natural phenomena also fall out of ecological balance. They protect the diversity of species and provide, even without legal regulations, wonderfully fragrant meadows with many flowers for nectar collecting insects such as (wild) bees and bumble bees, butterflies, rare beetles, etc. With their organic and ecological lifestyle-related and dietary

behaviour, they contribute a great deal to restoring the ecological balance in and between all natural phenomena on our planet.

3.5. Elemental reactions due to resource exploitation and pollution

Increased late frost, floods, heatwaves, hurricanes, violent storms, etc. and their ever more extreme effects **draw people's attention** to the exploitation of resources and pollution that are caused by disharmonies and imbalances of "giving and taking" and increasingly destroy the ecological balance of the elements (water, wood, fire, earth, metal/air). These are alarm signals, so that people change any of their social, sexual, nature-specific, lifestyle-related, dietary, consumer and decision-making behaviours that are not identical to the love residing within themselves and are imbued with disharmonies and imbalances of **"giving and taking"**.

A conventional farmer told me that he used to use his own seeds from the previous year's harvest for his pumpkin field and that mother plants with strong vine formations grew from these seeds. Convinced organic farmers still sow these old and self-bred seeds from the first pumpkins of mother plants today. After the late frost in 2016, many conventional farmers have realised that hybrid seeds can also be a disadvantage in conventionally managed farms because seed losses from hybrid seeds have a greater impact. Hybrid pumpkin seeds only produce bush plants **without vine formation**. Conventional farmers use hybrid seeds because all the pumpkins are ripe at the same time and efficient machine harvesting is possible. The seeds from hybrid pumpkins can **no longer produce offspring** next year because they have too little life and root forces. This is why conventional farmers have become dependent, every year anew, on the "hybrid seed offer" on the market.

3.6. Hybrid animals and hybrid seeds are being manipulated

A farmer told me that she had bought hybrid chicks specially bred for rapid growth and that she had not slaughtered a hen because she wanted to keep it

for the self-breeding of such chicks. Although the hen had a large garden at her disposal, she did not use the garden for a free life and natural eating behaviour (no longer saw or perceived the garden). She behaved like a "remote-controlled eating machine" because she was a victim of her manipulated life and eating behaviour. She hardly moved and only stood at the feeding trough until she could no longer stand up because of all the meat and fat she had put on. In the end, she had to be slaughtered out of necessity by the farmer. In this broiler chicken breeding (hybrid chicken breeding) fast growth (putting on meat) is the first priority. The feeding of the chickens with a special feed for "rapid growth" and their husbandry are designed in such a way that they move as little as possible and consume as few resources as possible for themselves. One reason why the hybrid hen did not adopt an eating behaviour that was "identical to her nature" was certainly her addictive eating behaviour from the fattening feed, which she was offered again and again in a feeding trough. If the farmer had scattered organic chicken feed on the ground for the hen, then the hen would have had to move while eating and would have been able to adopt a natural and species-appropriate eating behaviour more easily.
Meanwhile not only chickens, but also pigs and cattle are bred especially for putting on meat.

The species-appropriate, natural and strong root and life forces are lost more and more due to manipulations in hybrid seed and hybrid plant breeding. Hybrid plants can no longer reproduce themselves because they do not have enough **root and life forces** to do so. For this reason, hybrid seeds and hybrid plants and their fruits are not suitable for the preparation of root and life force-strengthening food. Such seeds and plants are offered by seed cultivation companies, nurseries and retailers in a "profit-oriented" manner—not only to conventional farmers, but also to hobby gardeners. My sister sowed pumpkin seeds from a beautiful and large pumpkin from last year's harvest that had grown on a hybrid plant. She was disappointed by the growth of the pumpkins and could not harvest a single edible pumpkin next year. Only mutilated and fungus infested small pumpkins without any resemblance to the previous year's pumpkins grew on the pumpkin plants.
Nevertheless, conventional farmers market their pumpkin seed oil from hybrid pumpkin seeds, which can no longer produce offspring, with a "seal of quality".

A few years ago, it was almost impossible to buy organic and untreated seeds and plants in retail businesses (supermarkets). Many hobby gardeners have therefore bred more and more organic seeds and plants themselves and exchanged rarities among themselves. The sale of untreated rarities (of plant diversity) was also severely restricted by legal regulations. Protests and the strong demand for organic seeds and plants have fortunately resulted in organic seeds and plants being offered for sale again in supermarkets. Probably also because rarity markets were heavily frequented. People who are convinced of ecological and organic farming only grow organic pure seed and organic plants in their gardens and on their fields—in a closed cycle and in the biorhythmic ecological balance of "giving and taking".

3.7. Genetically modified (GM) hybrid feed

A lot of experimentation (genetic manipulation) is going on especially with maize and soya beans (now with almost all seeds and unfortunately also with many animals) so that the feed for factory farming in conventional and streamlined farms can be grown as productively as possible. In a report on soya I read that herbivorous animals in the wild would not eat soya and that soya could trigger early puberty in girls and be a cause of infertility in men. In the past, organically grown and non-GM soya beans were used in menopausal women because of their harmonizing effect on the hormone balance.
Because of the large soya and maize fields for the factory farming of conventional farmers, there is no more **pure seed**. For this reason, I also distance myself from organic soya beans and organic maize.
The Chamber of Agriculture justifies the use of pesticides in conventional farming with advertising posters saying "no harvest without plant protection (euphemism for the use of pesticides)".
Only an ecological and organic dietary and consumer behaviour of many people can protect mankind from advertising statements such as "no offspring (children) without medication and food supplements".
In the list of ingredients of many products, especially finished products such as puddings, spreads, sweets, etc., you will find not only glutamates, flavour

enhancers, gluten, WGA (wheat germ agglutinins), preservatives, etc., but also maize and soya grown conventionally from hybrid seeds.

3.8. Trust in self-dynamic powers

Conventional farms, nurseries, orchards and vineyards have considerable additional costs due to the use of chemicals (artificial fertilisers, sprays).
Although a general conversion of all conventional farms to organic farms with green manuring has become urgently necessary, there are still barriers. In my living environment, the soils have very deep humus layers and therefore the best conditions for ecological and organic cultivation. I am convinced that all barriers will be overcome and that soon all farms, nurseries, orchards and vineyards will switch to organic farming.
By adopting ecological and organic farming practices, which are the best way to protect plants the environment, people will learn that all natural phenomena can regenerate and heal on their own, with their own dynamic powers and without external intervention, and that all natural phenomena are **perfectly, and comprehensively, coordinated in a closed cycle** and in biorhythmic ecological balance.
As a first measure, all schools for viticulture, fruit-growing, agriculture and horticulture should be **legally obliged to exclusively teach organic and ecological farming**. When converting conventional farms to organic farms, Chambers of Agriculture should provide farms with people who have experience with ecological and organic farming, especially with green manuring, and are able to maintain the balance of “giving and taking” (what the earth has given is **physically** returned to the earth) **in a closed cycle**.
The strong demand for organic food from many consumers helps to ensure that that retailers have to find more and more **producers for organically grown food**. Thus, conventional nurseries, farmers, fruit and wine growers will need to switch to organic and ecological farming in order to **secure their livelihoods for the future**.
In May 2018 it was published that already 24% of the arable land in Austria is organically farmed and that, if Austria's population would eat only 10% less meat, Austria could provide all people living here **with organic and healthy**

food at a regional level using the new arable land that would be available—provided that this land is farmed organically for direct food sources instead of using monocultures for animal feed.
Consumers with a conscious dietary and consumer behaviour can **control** producers, manufacturers and retailers (and not vice versa) so that "unhealthy and denatured food offers" will disappear from the shelves due to a lack of demand.

3.9. Only ecological and organic farming can maintain the ecological balance on our planet

Only ecological and organic farming can maintain the biorhythmic ecological balance in a comprehensively healthy growth, in a closed cycle and in the balance of "giving and taking".
A convinced organic farmer who is already 80 years old has explained to me that only ecologically and organically managed farms, nurseries, orchards and vineyards with green manuring can produce food that **strengthens life and root forces**. He told me that plants that are grown conventionally with artificial fertiliser only absorb a few nutrients (max. 12 to 14) from the artificial fertiliser. In contrast, organic plants from untreated seeds grown in humus with green manure absorb a variety of nutrients (up to 400) from the humus soil.
In conventionally managed farms and nurseries, plants and seeds are hardly provided with humus soil. In addition, only plants from hybrid seeds are grown there for fast growth, good appearance and high annual yield. Hybrid plants, which are grown with artificial fertilisers, all have deficiency symptoms. Thus, they are no longer in biorhythmic ecological balance and in a comprehensively healthy growth. "Pests" (actually beneficial organisms) perceive deficiency symptoms in conventionally grown plants and for them these plants are diseased organisms in the biorhythmic ecological balance. According to their task, they infest conventionally grown and diseased plants because they want to remove diseased organisms from the healthy biorhythmic ecological balance. The conventional farmer fights these "beneficial organisms" with

pesticides, which are then found by environmental organisations as pesticide residues in food.
In 2017, an environmental organisation found pesticide residues in four out of five commercially available apples tested, with the fifth apple being an organic apple. This organic farmer, who is convinced of organic farming, also told me about a potato experiment. In this experiment, the same organic potato variety was grown conventionally on a piece of field (using artificial fertiliser) and organically on the second half of the field (in humus with green manure). In this experiment, the potato beetles only infested potato plants that had been conventionally grown with artificial fertiliser. Not a single potato beetle could be found on the organically grown potato plants. This experiment proved that also the potato beetles only perform tasks for maintaining the biorhythmic ecological balance in a comprehensively healthy growth.
A few years ago, I bought potato rarities in a shop in autumn for the self-growing of such rarities and next year I planted them in my garden. I had to remove a rare variety from my garden soon after sprouting, because the potato haulm was infested with fungi and putrefactive bacteria. Although I had never come across a potato beetle in my garden before, the potato beetles infested the potato haulm of another rare potato variety. Nevertheless, the potato haulm from organic potatoes from the previous year's harvest planted in the same garden became neither sick nor infested with potato beetles. I suspect that the potato rarities I bought were not old and resistant potato varieties that had survived, but were bred for "profit-oriented sale".
My parents and grandparents told me that in the post-war period it was very difficult to get "healthy seeds" because of the famine. This could explain why, in the post-war period, the potato beetles introduced at that time infested the potato haulm, although no artificial fertiliser was available at that time.

3.10. Self-dynamic powers regenerate and heal

An experience with our peach tree, which has never in its life come into contact with artificial fertilisers or pesticides in the garden, strengthened my confidence in the self-dynamic powers in natural phenomena. A few years ago, all the leaves on our tree fell ill after it had sprouted in spring. So I directed my love towards the peach tree. The tree went into resonance with the love I directed towards him again and again and let go of the cause of the symptoms of its disease. Within ten days he dropped all the sick leaves and sprouted new healthy leaves and blossoms. In autumn and in the following years the tree gave us many healthy and beautiful fruits, so that we always had to preserve some of these delicious fruits for the winter. It is a misbelief when people think that organically grown vegetables and fruit cannot produce flawless fruits.

This report by Ulrich Arndt is intended to encourage "non-organic farmers" to convert their conventional farms to organic farms.
Our organism can free itself from tumour cells and cure cancer: All it needs are special, bioactive plant substances, which a naturally grown fruit, vegetable and cereal can provide—but nowadays almost only if it comes from organic farming. These special secondary plant substances that are part of the plant's natural defence mechanism are called salvestrols. They are formed when the plant is attacked by pathogens. If, for example, a fungus attacks a fruit, the plant forms a salvestrol specific for this pathogen at the site of attack, which is then found in the skin of the fruit and especially at the affected site. It is precisely these plant protective substances that we need in our food so that our organism can protect itself (e.g. against cancer). The fatal thing about it is: Conventionally grown fruit, vegetables, herbs and cereals are treated with artificial "plant-protection products" and therefore hardly form their own protective substances. Our current non-organic food contains very little or no salvestrols at all. It should actually contain more salvestrols than in the past and not less, because the amount of environmental toxins is increasing more and more, and even the synthetic pesticide residues themselves act on our body as an additional stress factor. The only remedy is a consistent switch to organic food.

3.11. Draw knowledge from gardening experience

I draw many insights from my own garden experiences and observations. Although there were red snails around my garden time and again, they did neither infest the organic plants growing in the garden nor their organic fruits.

I provide a lot of living space for earwigs so that there is no problem with lice in the garden. For pollination I attract (wild) bees and bumble bees with a variety of flowers between the beds. Euphorbia plants prevent voles from settling in the garden. In autumn, harvested beds are covered with hay. The soil then remains moist and soft and cats do not use my garden beds as a toilet. Two years ago, I set up a huge straw bale for "growing potatoes without soil" (an experimental project) in the outer area of my garden. Since the potato project did not work, I wanted to grow pumpkins on this straw bale infested with putrefactive bacteria and moulds in the second year on organic soil heaped up in the hollow of the bale. The pumpkin plants in the middle of the straw bale were sickly despite the humus soil and I could only harvest a few small pumpkins. A little further away, pumpkins grew on a three-year-old compost heap with pure humus soil in full splendour and completely healthily. Based on this experience, I make sure that plants no longer come into contact with putrefactive bacteria and moulds. I only use green grass clippings for mulching on very hot days and very thinly laid so that the grass can dry quickly and the ground remains **permeable to air**. Otherwise, I use dry organic hay, organic sheep's wool and selected medicinal herbs, such as yarrow, horsetail, stinging nettles, dandelion, ground ivy ... Mulching with organic material improves the soil and keeps the soil moist and loose on the surface. As a result, the plants are well nourished and protected from drying out. Such plants rarely or not at all need to be watered. All plants, including trees and shrubs, love organic sheep's wool.

In the course of the garden year, much organic mulch material on air-permeable soil is decomposed by soil life (macroorganisms and microorganisms) to humus without rotting. The king of the macroorganisms in soil life is the earthworm, which eats organic material and, with its excretion, provides the plants with nutritious (earthworm) humus from mulch material for a healthy growth in a very short time.

Please do not break up the soil (turn it from bottom to top) in spring or autumn, as the sensitive soil life comes to the surface and dies during the breaking process. If you have covered the soil again and again with organic mulch material during the garden year, there will almost be no need to till the garden beds in spring. A garden claw will be sufficient to loosen up the soil.

The sowing of green manure seeds between the rows of cultivated plants or in late summer after harvesting on beds covers the soil. Uncovered soil is like an

open wound for the soil and for soil life. The organic substance of the green manure revitalises soil life and thus improves the structure and aeration of the soil. When I extend garden areas, I plant the non-hardy blue or narrow-leaf lupin in the first year. It is a papilionaceous plant with pulses and therefore a nitrogen collector. The blue lupin has very deep roots and even breaks up soil compacted by construction machinery and tractors. I remove green manure plants that have not yet decomposed from the beds in spring and compost them. Then you have wonderful humus soil which you can use for growing young plants in pots.
When I notice that plants are sickly, I use medicinal herbs for mulching. I follow my intuition when selecting the herbs. You can also put herbs such as stinging nettles, yarrow, horsetail, etc. in a tub, pour water over them and enrich the water with the nutrients and minerals of the herbs. I leave the herbal medicinal water only one day before putrefactive bacteria colonise the water. I do not think much of stinking liquid manure (liquid nettle manure), which is already in the process of decaying. Cultivated plants (such as pepper, tomato, cucumber, pumpkin plants ...), which are watered with this medicinal water, recover and the leaves on the plants soon show up again in a rich green.
I leave fallen leaves under the trees in autumn. The fallen leaves, which are decomposed by the soil life to a nutrient-rich humus, nourish the tree next year from spring to autumn. Deciduous trees nourish themselves **in a closed cycle** in the biorhythmic ecological balance and in a comprehensively healthy growth. Since we have pruned back our apple trees from the beginning in spring, many water sprouts are formed every year, which we cut off in spring, process into wood chips and make available to the trees again for their healthy growth by distributing the wood chips among the trees. By late summer, even these wood chips have been decomposed by soil life.
In a state of (self-)awareness, (self-)perception and (self-)knowledge, realising that **love is the cause of all beings and life itself**, all natural phenomena, including humans, **nourish themselves out of the power source of light and love residing within themselves "in a closed cycle" and with strong and all-encompassing life and root forces**.
Those who have reached this level of awareness only eat what has been organically and ecologically grown **in a closed cycle, in the balance of "giving and taking"** and in the biorhythmic ecological balance, or what has grown on

its own in nature, because only such foods **strengthen the life and root forces** for a comprehensively healthy growth.
By organically and ecologically cultivating my vegetable garden, my fruit trees and my berries and by maintaining the balance of “giving and taking”, I harvest every year many beautiful and perfectly healthy fruits and garden gifts. It is a misbelief when people think that organic fruits, organic vegetables and organic herbs cannot be flawless. The opposite is true. The taste and the fragrance are unsurpassable and the vibration is **identical to the love residing within oneself**.
I get many garden tips from my youngest daughter, who has a very special relationship to animals and plants. In the garden and around the house you feel like in a “paradise”. You can admire a variety of flowers, plants and butterflies as well as rare beetles and observe how wild bees, bumble bees and honey bees turn somersaults together in calyxes. She cultivates plants that are threatened with extinction and breeds (medicinal) plants that can hardly be found in the wild any more. She told me that young plants, which are produced from roots, are nourished by the mother plant, similar to mammals via the umbilical cord. She also observes the social behaviour of plants. She always plants siblings next to each other, because these young plants (trees, shrubs, vegetable plants, etc.) do not compete, grow in a good social behaviour and even feed each other. All seeds she sows in a bed come from the same mother plant.
Once a calabash plant, which rose itself, settled down next to a chayote planted by me. The calabash (a plant from another pumpkin family), which produced beautiful fruits, engaged in extreme competition with the chayotes, which I had planted there. It claimed a very large growth space just for itself and overgrew everything that was growing next to it. This is why the chayote harvest this year was very poor.

When I visited my daughter in August 2017, she was in a desperate state, because at the beginning of August many nectar-collecting insects, like wild bees, bumble bees and rare beetles, had suddenly disappeared from her garden. My attempt to calm her down with the hope that the wild bees and bumble bees might have withdrawn earlier this year failed. This phenomenon I have experienced myself in my garden and in my living environment.

In autumn 2017, conventional farmers were able to reap a sensational hybrid pumpkin harvest because many nectar-collecting insects were increasingly attracted to the pumpkin blossoms on the hybrid pumpkin plants due to the ever weaker supply of wild plants. Although maize is pollinated by the wind, insects fly to maize plans (including hybrid maize) in order to drink the condensation water accumulated under the axils of the maize leaves. The wild bees and bumble bees probably died of an immune deficiency due to the contact with pesticides and environmental toxins. Hopefully the queen bees have produced offspring for next spring before they died and hopefully the brood of bumble bees and wild bees will survive the winter.

3.12. Honeybees

My elder sister has a lot of experience with honeybees because her husband was a beekeeper and she became a beekeeper herself after his death. She told me that honeybees were very peaceful insects and that 15 years ago her husband could still work without protective clothing and veil. Since beekeepers thought that more aggressive bees provide a higher yield and have a stronger immune system, they bred such bees. This is why beekeepers today can only approach their bee colony with protective clothing and veils. Meanwhile attempts are being made to breed more peaceful bees again. Such attempts fail, if the bee colony does not accept the new queen bee and kills it. As soon as there is no queen bee left in the hive, a larva in a queen bee cell in the hive is fed royal jelly by the bees so that the larva develops into a queen bee. Other larvae are raised with flower pollen and nectar.
Manipulative interventions in natural phenomena destroy the balance and harmony in the natural phenomenon and between natural phenomena. Many beekeepers are confronted again and again with the mass mortality of their bees. This is certainly also due to the fact that bees, which no longer find any biological plant species diversity, also visit blossoms on hybrid plants, which have almost no life and root forces left in them. In addition, nectar collecting insects are also confronted with immunocompromising pesticides and environmental toxins. Another reason for the immunodeficiency of honeybees is that highly profit-oriented, conventional beekeepers take away almost all

the self-collected food from honeybees. As a feed substitute, they get denatured sugar water without natural life and root forces. My sister only takes honey from the combs until mid-August and leaves the feed collected by her bee colony from August to the end of September in the hive during the winter. With this approach and a lot of love, her bee colonies almost always survive the winter with no major damage.

3.13. Cultured microorganisms

"Effective microorganisms" (EM) prevent mould infestation. EM are used in the garden, in the household (washing clothes, cleaning, etc.) and with animals against fleas, ticks, mites, etc. in households and also often on organic farms. Effective microorganisms are small organisms that can be either lactic acid bacteria or yeast fungi or photosynthetic bacteria. In the wild, these organisms decompose dead organisms **in a decay process** back to earth. This happens in the biorhythmic ecological balance and in a comprehensively healthy growth.
Although cultured "effective microorganisms" are advertised as being a natural "superpower" against fungal attacks, etc., no one knows yet what effects this "superpower" produced in a laboratory or at home will have in organisms and in the genes of organisms, especially in the natural microorganisms in beings (microbiomes) and in soil life.
For digestion, humans enter into a symbiosis with natural microorganisms (e.g. in digestive enzymes). Thus, the microorganisms produced in a laboratory for the food and pharmaceutical industries and those cultured by the farmers themselves could have harmful effects on the symbiosis (microbiomes) in beings and destructive effects on soil life.
Fungi, photosynthetic and lactic acid bacteria decompose dead matter, including undigested matter in human intestines, in a decay process that produces decay gases and toxins.
At a lecture on ecological and organic gardening I was shocked when the speaker explained that she uses EM in her organic nursery. She also uses EM for "fast composting" by inoculating the compost with it and then covering the compost hermetically with "plastic".

I would never perform fast, non-air-permeable composting with cultured effective microorganisms, because when covering the compost with plastic no **air-permeable** natural composting with the species-rich soil life (natural microorganisms and macroorganisms) and without the formation of rot is possible.
Microorganisms cannot be seen with the naked eye. Nevertheless, like macroorganisms (humans, animals, plants) they are living beings. In my opinion, effective microorganisms (living beings) cultured in the laboratory or at home are neither suitable for growing organic fruit and vegetables nor for cleaning and washing nor for pets—also for ethical reasons.

4.1. Self-dynamic powers in beings

In all natural phenomena, including humans, the effect of the same forces and laws can be observed. All natural phenomena are perfectly, and **comprehensively, coordinated** in the biorhythmic ecological balance, **while nourishing the power of light and love**, and should never have been changed by humans. Agglutinins and gluten probably only became part of cereals after humans had manipulated the original grain by breeding (up to genetic manipulation).
When my second grandson was born, a vast amount of ground elder spread over my natural meadow, protected by a walnut tree. My daughter ate this natural gift at least two times a week in a spinach or soup. In the postpartum period, these greens provided my daughter with iron and, above all, stimulated milk production so that she could fully breastfeed her son for more than a year.
The elements (water, wood, fire, earth, metal/air), which are the first natural phenomena and which are present in all other natural phenomena, act **with their elemental forces in all natural phenomena**.
The elemental energy flows (meridians) of the elements in the subtle and gross bodies provide natural phenomena with energies, vibrations and emotions of the **power of light and love** from the abundance and fullness of the **power source of light and love residing within themselves, "online" and "free to the door"—in the biorhythmic ecological balance**, for their comprehensively

healthy growth and in the flow of being and living, where, in all energy flows, **exclusively love flows freely in a closed cycle**.
The acupuncture or acupressure points are opening points in the meridian system with important functions on the body surface where energies, vibrations and emotions can be reached in the energy flow.
Regular meridian stretching exercises, daily rubbing of the skin, daily tapping of the body and a lifestyle and diet that are identical to oneself contribute a lot to the free flow of all energies in the subtle and gross bodies.
Shiatsu or acupuncture treatments also make energies flow again and are a good prophylaxis for the immune system.

The water element

The element of water is assigned to the bladder and kidney. The bladder and kidneys maintain the fluid balance of the body and are responsible for cleansing and regulation. The basic themes of water include libido, courage, deep life crises, leadership qualities, good hearing, good teeth and bones, offspring, a healthy handling of stress, vitality, willpower and (self-)safety. Vitality (water) nourishes creativity (wood). The calm in the water supports the centred and concentrated execution in the wood element (the gallbladder energy). Water needs clarity and direction from the metal element. Vitality, tranquillity and the harmonious flow in the water can be created through structure and order. People with an comprehensively healthy water are gentle, courageous, proactive, capable of relating and of handling relationships, calm and relaxed. They have a calm gaze and maintain eye contact. Their voice is calm and clear and their posture powerful and upright. They also have a lot of (self-)confidence and stable relationships.
The water element controls birth and dying in cycles of being and living in a self-dynamic and automated way. However, the colon energy in the metal element is responsible for letting go of the drawn and one's own physical dense matter.
The kidney is the **"root of life"**. The water kidney is responsible for the acid-base balance and the fire kidney for the hormone balance. The kidney stores the essence, accommodates the willpower and governs birth, growth,

reproduction and development. It produces the marrow, fills the brain and bones, manifests itself in the hair and is responsible for good hearing, healthy ears and, together with the spleen, blood formation.
The bladder stores and excretes urine. The bladder energy controls the function of the autonomic nervous system and is closely linked to the pituitary gland, which controls the endocrine system. The bladder (executor) distributes energy and brings energy to where it is needed. Furthermore, the bladder has an influence on sexuality as well as on the function of the uterus and the prostate gland.

The wood element

The liver and gallbladder are assigned to the element of wood. The main activity time of the wood energy in the biorhythm is between 1:00 am and 3:00 am. People with a healthy wood energy live out their creativity, vocations and talents identically to themselves, autonomously and self-reliantly, and with a secure income and livelihood. Their communication is clear and easy to understand. Even if they are active at night, they are still awake in the morning. The spring, the morning hours and the life phases of childhood and youth are assigned to the wood element. The cardinal direction of the wood energy is the east with the rising sun. A healthy and strong wood energy can be recognised by the shine of the nails and by a harmoniously fulfilled sexuality. Wood energy flows upwards and is growth and development. Those who are not in balance with wood energy are very sensitive to wind. In such a situation you have to protect your neck from wind and draught. Wood energy is the energy of continuous development and movement. If development, movement, creativity, talents and vocations are suppressed, the wood energy can stagnate and this can lead to acute attacks of aggression as well as migraine, manic and autoimmune diseases. All drugs destroy the free flow of wood energy as well as a person's identity and individuality. Tenosynovitis draws people's attention to accumulated wood energy and inflexibility. If people are absorbed in doing something with fun and joy and without "time pressure", then their wood energy is flowing freely.

Stable water makes the wood flexible and lively. You are then in a position to plan with clear goals and to execute what you have planned. Since a healthy and freely flowing wood energy sets clear steps, the impulsive expression is often very loud, but the communication is nevertheless clear and distinct with targeted messages. If people are in harmony with their wood energy, they maintain direct eye contact.
The liver is the largest detoxification organ in the body and can only store blood during rest periods. If the liver is overburdened (overstrained), it can only recover by lying down. Overconsumption of alcohol or other drugs makes the liver sick and the behaviour manic. Alcoholics or drug addicts very often suffer from hopelessness and stagnation. If aggression, rage and anger are suppressed again and again, then it can come to an extreme discharge of the accumulated wood energy (running amok).
The liver energy is the architect and responsible for (life) planning and the gallbladder energy is the energy executing the plans. But people also need the "organisation" of metal energy (the organisational talent) for execution. In relation to the goal, the liver is stubborn. However, the gallbladder energy is flexible in the actions (in the execution). The colour is green, the smell is rancid and the taste sour. The strengths in wood in the biorhythmic ecological balance and in a comprehensively healthy growth are as follows: vitality, determination, well-functioning joints, good tension in tendons and ligaments, relaxation, composure, good eyes, planning ability, flexible execution, (self-)responsibility, independence and autonomy. If wood energy is blocked, people can be irascible, quick-tempered, angry, sensitive to noise, jealous and frustrated. Visual disturbances, yellowing of the eyes or skin, strokes, impotence, frigidity, headaches or nausea may also occur.

The fire element

The power of fire unfolds at noon, in summer and in the prime of life. The colour of the fire element is red, the sense organ is the tongue with speaking in a clear voice, the smell is burned, the taste is bitter and the body fluid is sweat. With a free-flowing fire energy people go through life with a lot of joy, fun and ease (laughing and dancing). The fire energy controls the ability to give and receive love. If the fire in people is out of balance, then people want control over everything. This is why they take everything into their own hands. Delegating tasks and responsibility is extremely difficult for them in such situations. The consequences are the feeling of being overwhelmed and permanent stress with health problems through to heart attacks. Too much fire energy in the heart triggers rapid, incomprehensible speaking or stuttering and excessive sweating due to nervous tension. When the fire in people is in balance, it produces joy, fulfilment and a harmonious exchange of giving and taking. The eyes of these people shine, they have kindness, generosity and good taste. They are characterised by good leadership qualities and always know when to delegate tasks and responsibility. When they have reached the autumn of their lives, they withdraw to leave their place (position) to younger people.

In primary fire, the heart and small intestine are assigned to the fire element. The cardiovascular system and the triple warmer belong to the secondary fire. In the biorhythm, the small intestine energy is active between 1:00 and 3:00 pm. In the small intestine, food is processed and the nutrients are formed and transferred into the blood. In shock situations, the energy of the small intestine is the first protector of the heart. In the case of sudden shocks or fears (e.g. exam nerves), the small intestine energy channels shocks and fear-inducing energies out of the organism through diarrhoea.

In case of an imbalance of the small intestine, strong feelings such as anger or feelings of guilt can no longer be expressed and so fatigue, pain in the shoulder area, neck and back, leg cramps, migraine attacks and menstrual problems or an irregular bowel movement occur. The organ and energy states of the small intestine can be seen on the upper and lower lip or in the corners of the mouth. Inflammations that are present in the corners of the mouth reflect inflammations of the small intestine. Imbalances and disharmonies in the energy of the small intestine express themselves in an emotionally charged and explosive state and above all in a weakness in decision-making. When the small intestine energy is in harmony and balance, pure and clear identity- and individuality-based decisions are made.

Like the cardiovascular system, the triple warmer belongs to the secondary fire. It governs all protective functions in our body and, like the small intestine energy, is a protector of the heart. When the protective energy (the triple warmer) flows freely, people (beings) are protected when changes, including time zone changes, or external influences and attacks occur. The three combustion chambers are coordinated by the triple warmer. The organs in the chest, the lungs and the heart form the "upper warmer", the first power source (combustion chamber), which is responsible for breathing and the cardiovascular system. The upper abdominal cavity with the liver, gallbladder, stomach and spleen form the "medium warmer" and hence the second power source. The medium combustion chamber is responsible for digestion and also for absorbing and digesting impressions. The "lower warmer", the third power source, contains the sex organs, large intestine, small intestine, bladder and kidney, which are responsible for the excretions and for sexuality. With nourishing and protective energy, the triple warmer regulates the distribution of nutrients to the extremities by controlling the peripheral circulation and the "heating system" in the body. Imbalances and disharmonies in the triple warmer manifest themselves in a defensive attitude to life and in the inability to interact with other people, but also in a tense and stiff body with clenched fists. Those affected react hypersensitively to changes in their environment. When they react to fluctuations in temperature and humidity, the nasal and neck mucosa as well as the lymph glands are swollen. Allergies, colds, chest pressure, itchy skin, being excessively ticklish, hypersensitivity to pain, eczema and hives are often common reactions. In the balanced state, the triple warmer produces sustainability. It then expresses the feelings.

The earth element

The stomach and the spleen with the pancreas are assigned to the earth element. These organs and their energies are responsible for the absorption and digestion (both physical and mental) of food and information. The main activity time of the stomach in the biorhythm is between 7:00 am and 9:00 am, and that of the spleen between 9:00 am and 11:00 am. The season is late summer. The colours of the earth are brown, yellow and orange, the orifice is the mouth, the sense is tasting, the smell is musty, the taste is sweet, the body fluid is saliva and beauty features are lips, tissues and muscles. In a harmonious earth energy people are likable and trustful. They have good common sense, good ideas, a sense of humour and can think logically. An imbalance in the

earth energy can lead to cravings for sweets, a feeling of cold in the back or hips, loose stools, bruises, lack of exercise, weight problems, jealousy, distrust and scepticism. Although the relationships in the earth element focus primarily on the family and closer circle of friends, the earth energy controls all relationships in singledom and coupledom, as well as in professional, business, leisure and social life. People are often powerless and restless because they are overly precise, brood over things, have an exaggerated thirst for knowledge or worry excessively (often unnecessarily). Physical symptoms then usually occur in the middle of the back, around the shoulder blades, in the knees, in the prostate gland, uterus and breasts or during menstruation.
The stomach is the authority that stores and manages food, thoughts and ideas for later use. In a healthy earth energy, "giving and taking" in relationships are in balance. The spleen energy is responsible for the ability to relate and handle relationships and the stomach energy is responsible for separations.
An important task of the spleen is the production of energy from food and the transport of liquids. A lack of digestive juices leads to a dry and sticky feeling in the mouth. The spleen energy controls all areas where digestive enzymes are produced, such as the mouth, stomach, small intestine and gallbladder, but also the hormone production in women. In the lymphatic system, the spleen energy fulfils the task of keeping the fluid in the channels and in the body system and keeping organs in place. The cause of swollen lymph nodes and increased salivation is often a weak spleen energy. People with a balanced and strong spleen energy have a practical understanding and intelligence and can improvise well (make a lot out of little). These people have strong life and root forces in their identity- and individuality-based behaviour, are stable and strong in their midst and have both feet firmly on the ground.
The stomach reflects the fatherly relationship with one's father and with one's own children. The spleen reflects the motherly relationship with one's mother and with one's own children. Fertility and conception need a harmonious and balanced earth energy.

The metal element

The lungs and colon are assigned to the element of metal/air. The main activity time of the lungs in the biorhythm is between 3:00 am and 5:00 am, and that of the colon between 5:00 am and 7:00 am. The west, the cardinal direction of the setting sun, and the autumn, where nature gradually withdraws and collects its forces in the roots, are assigned to metal energy. In a healthy metal energy, people withdraw in the autumn of their lives with a clear approach to maintaining distance. The colours of metal are pale, white and ash-grey, the orifice is the nose, the sense is the smell, the characteristics are the body hair and the tissue of the skin. When the voice is in disharmony, it is whiny and whimpering. The smell is rutted, pungent or medicinal and the taste of the metal is sharp. The body fluid is the mucus. The metal energy enables structure and order and the emotion is grief. The colon energy is the energy of letting go of stools, (self-)blockages, (self-)destruction, traumas, fears, addictions ...

In a harmonious lung energy, people draw from the abundance of their possibilities with insight, far-sightedness and overview to develop their creativity, talents and vocations. The central theme of the metal element is the confrontation between proximity (allowing proximity) and distance (the clear dissociation with clearly defined limits). The process of cutting the cord in the biorhythm is controlled self-dynamically by the water energy, and the colon energy makes letting go (cutting the cord) possible.

The lungs are reflected in the breathing, in the nose and chest areas. A distinction is made between two breathing types: The inhalation types (state of fullness) hold on inwardly, are dogmatic (right/wrong), critical, neat, clean, cynical, preach, do not let go of energies, and are often uptight because of a lack of lightness. However, despite the inner stiffness, they can be physically flexible and stretchy. In exhalation types (state of emptiness) the shoulder falls forward. These people are often melancholic, depressed and in need of others. They cling to others because they need something from other people all the time. The preservation of dissociation and distance must be demanded of these people, because they often have no respect for the space of other people and cross the line again and again.

The strengths in the metal element can be seen in a good organisation, in a clear and analytical mind, in good social contacts, in openness for new things,

changes and development, in a fundamentally positive attitude, in a sense of justice, in being communicative, honest, respectful and orderly, but also in taking initiatives and in good powers of resistance with a strong immune system.
Imbalances and disharmonies in the metal element can be recognised by a weak, often transparent or dry skin and a skin susceptible to skin diseases, a pale face, an often congested nose, laborious and restricted breathing, asthma, bronchitis, coughs, colds, depression, dejectedness, melancholy, the feeling of being overwhelmed, shy behaviour, little social interest, claustrophobia, being caught up within oneself and in one's own structures, stubbornness, stiffness in the back and shoulder areas and poor powers of resistance due to a weak immune system.

If all elements (water, wood, fire, earth, metal/air) are **comprehensively coordinated and in harmony and balance, while nourishing the power of light and love**—"in the here and now", in and between all beings, in all places of being and living and in all relationships, situations and communication within themselves, as well as between themselves and all beings and life itself, in the biorhythmic ecological balance, in a comprehensively healthy growth and in the flow of being and living—, the harmony and balance of the elements will be reflected in all natural phenomena, in the full physical, mental and spiritual well-being and in soul, family and world peace.

4.2. Tasks of the immune system

The immune system has the task of bringing beings into harmony **with the environment of their food sources**. When people eat tropical fruits in a cold climate, their immune system wants to bring them into harmony with the hot climate (where the fruits have grown). If the climate and environmental conditions of the food sources are not identical to the climate and environmental conditions of the beings, the immune system in beings will get confused and will lose its bearings. If people repeatedly eat food that is not identical to the climate and the specific conditions of their environment, their immune system will become weaker and weaker. The consequences are food intolerances and diseases. Only **seasonal and regional** organic food that strengthens life and root forces and is in line with the seasonal **biorhythm** brings people into **biorhythmic ecological balance**. Fruits that grow in a very hot climate form a lot of cooling energies within themselves so that they can withstand the hot climate. When people eat such fruits, the coolness from this food enters their blood. In the cold season, however, the organism needs more internal warmth again. If people have had a lot of cooling food (tropical fruits, ice cream, yoghurt ...) in summer and even in autumn, they get a runny nose as soon as the temperature falls or they have to empty their bladder very often because the coolness has to be eliminated from the organism again. In order to excrete the coolness via the mucus, they pick up viruses and bacteria from their environment. The cold is over in a few days when the immune system in people is strong enough, enabling self-regeneration and self-healing. The heat balance in the organism has then adapted to the cold season again. If the immune system is weakened as a result of stress and strong exploitation of resources or if the organism is overacidified due to improper diet, the viruses and bacteria picked up from outside will perceive the organism as a "sick organism" which is no longer in the biorhythmic ecological balance and no longer in a comprehensively healthy growth. These pathogens will begin to multiply very quickly because they want to remove "diseased matter" from the ecological balance in accordance with their task. The organism will defend itself against these attacks by causing a fever. All beings in a state of illness need rest, the feeling of security and enough time for self-regeneration and self-healing (slow is faster). It feels very good when, as soon as body, mind or soul send out alarm signals (symptoms), you completely withdraw and allow yourself to rest and recuperate.

Ill beings intuitively reduce their food intake so that more resources are available for self-regeneration and self-healing. TCM teaches that "a healthy gut means a healthy human being". That is why in TCM the nutrition is always adapted to the state of health. As a first measure in case of symptoms and also during the regeneration period, people following TCM often only consume "rice congee" (a healing food from TCM), because this healing food consumes almost no resources for digestion and provides the organism with fast and gentle energy. Rice congee is also an ideal stomach protector when medication is used to treat symptoms.

Preparation of rice congee: Put 1 cup of Seewinkler regional organic short-grain rice (from Seewinkel in Burgenland) into a sieve and wash out all impurities from the rice under the sink with hot water. Bring the clean rice to the boil with 10 cups of water in a cooking pot. Turn down to the lowest heat and let the rice porridge simmer lightly for 3 to 4 hours. Stir the porridge again and again during cooking. Fill the congee into ¼ l screw cap jars while it is still hot, allow it to cool and store it in the refrigerator. Always warm up the rice congee before eating.

Healing food with regional organic golden millet: Rinse 1 cup of organic golden millet and optionally 2 tablespoons of whole-grain millet for adults vigorously with hot water under the sink, bring the millet to the boil with 3 cups of water and let it simmer lightly over the lowest heat for half an hour. After cooking, either press the millet porridge through a sieve or drive it through a straining machine so that the husks can be removed from the whole grain golden millet. The rest of the procedure is the same as for the rice congee. I mix sugar-free apple or pear sauce with the millet porridge for children or for people who do not want to eat the millet pudding in its pure form.

In all diseases and especially in colds, bronchitis or inflammation of the bladder, patients have to drink a lot of fluids. When sick people regain their appetite and hunger, they should be offered **seasonal and regional** organic food that strengthens their life and root forces and is in line with the seasonal **biorhythm** (see nutrition plan). My mother always let us children have a fever for three days and gave us a lot to drink and only light food. She only consulted a doctor if the fever had not gone down after three days. I felt her tender loving care to be very healing when she laid her hands on painful areas or held my forehead while I was vomiting.

4.3. What is the biorhythm?

From the moment of incarnation, the **powerful vibration of one's own light and love** also manifests itself in a gross body. Everything is vibration and all vibrations are subject to an order that is **identical to the love within ourselves**.

If we fall out of this order (vibration), then we are no longer in the biorhythmic ecological balance.
If the subtle and gross bodies, the mind and the soul **vibrate with the power of their own light and love**, beings are "in the here and now", in the biorhythmic ecological balance, in peace and in harmony within themselves, as well as between themselves and all beings and life itself, in a comprehensively healthy growth and in the flow of being and living, where, in all energy flows, **exclusively love flows freely in a closed cycle**, in the biorhythm of being and living and in the **biorhythm** of seasons, day and night that is identical to the love residing within themselves.
If beings do not have a day and night **biorhythm** adapted to the season, then deep relaxation and deep sleep at night and creative power during the day are in disharmony.
Parents are greatly challenged when their baby sleeps through the day and is awake at night. Only if babies, the elderly or people in need of care are able to follow an order **(a rhythm)** in their nutrition, care and activities, is there a very good chance that they will get into a deep relaxation at night and regenerate in deep sleep and that they will be relaxed and balanced during the day.
Of course, there can be individual deviations in the biorhythm of beings, since no single being is comparable with another being in its uniqueness. Fingerprints are therefore also suitable for the identification of people because they reflect their uniqueness.
Organs in the body also follow a biorhythm and are only particularly active at certain times. Since, according to their biorhythm, the digestive organs are no longer active at night, food should not be consumed late in the evening or at night. According to its biorhythm, the large intestine of humans usually "wakes up" between 5:00 am and 7:00 am for defaecation. In the morning the stomach is ready for food intake again only between 7 am and 9 am, and so on. Life and root force-strengthening organic food (a healthy breakfast) eaten in line with the physical biorhythm, i.e. between 7:00 am and 9:00 am, is easily and efficiently metabolised, providing the organism with many life and root forces for daily activities.

4.4. Living in line with the seasonal biorhythm

According to the seasonal biorhythm, the days (exposure to sunlight) are shorter and the nights (darkness) are longer in winter. Beings use the longer nights for the regeneration according to the seasonal biorhythm. Trees drop their leaves in late autumn and their sap withdraws into the roots. In the animal world many animals hibernate and do not wake up until spring. When people have adapted their lifestyle and eating habits to the seasonal **biorhythm**, they take enough time in winter to regenerate their body, mind and soul. The life and root forces are then strengthened for a **more active** life in spring.

If, according to the seasonal **biorhythm** and under natural storage conditions, there are no more regional and seasonal organic vegetable supplies available, then the time has come for the organism to adjust to a few foods.

The self-purifying, self-regenerating and self-healing powers are particularly active during this time. Until spring I then eat, according to the seasonal **biorhythm**, the still available life and root force-strengthening regional and seasonal foods, such as organic buckwheat, organic millet, organic beans, organic lentils, organic nuts, preserved and dried fruits from the previous year's harvest and—as long as there are still organic apples and organic waxy potatoes available under natural storage conditions—also apples and potatoes. Because I go to bed earlier during winter dormancy, two meals a day are enough for me during this time.

Only in spring, when the body, mind and soul perceive the spring awakening and the scent of wild garlic, dandelion, stinging nettles ... in the environment of their living space again, the organism and the microbiome within the organism (which always adapt to the regional and seasonal food supply according to the seasonal **biorhythm**) are ready again to ingest more food from the regional and seasonal food supply.

More and more people suffer from burnout because they no longer live in line with the **seasonal biorhythm**. The shorter days given to us by nature are completely ignored, especially in the business world. In the shopping centres and at many Christmas markets, artificial light turns night into day. This is why people are often exposed to even more digital and electromagnetic waves in

the winter months. More resources instead of less are consumed in winter. Many people, although they should be resting, rush from one shop and from one Christmas market to another.
Even in the country it is hardly possible to enjoy the peace and the darkness of the longer nights during this time, because every village and many families would like to have the "most beautiful Christmas lighting" with many glitter effects and very bright light on their houses and in their gardens.

5.1. Eat a diet that is identical to yourself

In the macrobiotic cuisine of Asian origin, people eat seasonal and regional food that strengthens their life and root forces with 70% of cereals (preferably rice), 20% of vegetable protein and 10% of seasonal and regional vegetables and fruit.
The seeds used in the macrobiotic cuisine to strengthen life and root forces, especially the legumes, such as beans, lentils and chickpeas, quickly take root due to their strong life and root forces when they are inserted into the soil and watered. If you consume organically grown vegetable protein instead of animal protein, you will draw **strong life and root forces from the direct source of protein** for a comprehensively healthy growth.
In the macrobiotic cuisine, which is largely in line with TCM and its teaching "a healthy gut means a healthy you", milk and sugar are not used for health reasons.
After my macrobiotic training I took on the macrobiotic diet, using recipes from macrobiotic cookbooks. Soon I realised that the non-regional ingredients in the recipes were not in harmony with the environment in which I live.
For this reason and taking into account the environment in which I live, I switched my diet with the macrobiotic approach to the "macrobiotic, **regional and seasonal**" organic diet that is in line with the seasonal **biorhythm**.

5.2. The effect of food on your organism

Everything you ingest, take and assimilate, also through your diet, has an effect on your body, mind and soul, but also on relationships, situations and communication between yourself and all beings and life itself.
Alcohol, sugar, tropical luxury foods and drinks (coffee, etc.), fresh dairy products, milk, fruit and raw foods have an expanding effect on your organism. Meat, eggs, cheese, salty foods, fish as well as baked, roasted and toasted foods have a contracting effect on your organism.
But there are also foods, such as organic millet, organic buckwheat, organic natural rice or organic pumpkins ..., which, instead of having a contracting or expanding effect, have a harmonising effect on your organism (in the subtle and gross bodies), on your mind, on your soul and on relationships, situations and communication.
Those who prefer food with a contracting effect, such as much meat and foods baked in the oven (bread, cakes, etc.), often have very tense fasciae, muscles and organs (the pancreas is particularly affected), because meat and baked foods have a strongly contracting effect. This effect can also be felt in relationships, situations and communication. Those who eat too much food with an expanding effect, often have weak muscles. Since these people usually have too little root force within themselves, there is often no ground beneath their feet.

5.3. Foods and drinks that have become everyman's drugs

Animal milk is a foreign substance in the human organism

It is not intended by nature that humans or animals should consume milk from other species. Milk from other species is a foreign substance in the organism and weakens the immune system. Milk consumption can be the cause of many diseases. Milk is often the cause of mucous congestion in the intestines and lungs.

On conventional and often on organic farms with livestock, cows are only a production unit in the barn. Once one has looked into the sad eyes of a dairy cow, which is completely exploited and emaciated to the bone, one never again wants to be a contributor (consumer of meat and milk) to such exploitations.
Only as long as the suckler cow and the calf are together on the pasture or in the barn in suckler cow husbandry is the world still alright for the calf and for the suckler cow. I always get very sad when, usually after the sixth month, the calf is taken from the suckler cow, and the suckler cow cries very loudly and full of pain for her calf. If the calf, which also bellows for its mother and its family, comes into a fattening farm, it is marketed as veal up to the age of one year or later as beef. Dairy cows have an even worse fate, because the calf is taken from them immediately after calving. The cow as a production unit in the barn must be a milk supplier again soon after calving and also deliver the next calf again. These cows produce milk and carry a calf to term at the same time. The life of these cows is very time-limited due to extreme exploitation. If they can no longer produce, exploited and emaciated to the bone, they end up on a slaughtering block, preferably for sausage and *Leberkäse* (beef and pork loaf) production. Consumers of such meat products receive the energies, vibrations and emotions of completely exploited and **very sad** cows and the waste products of slaughtered pigs.

Sugar has become everyman's drug in the last 200 years

If, during the preparation of food, additional sugar or honey, maple syrup ... are added to fruit, vegetables or cereals with natural fructose, the pancreas is overburdened with the processing of the added sugar.
Overconsumption of sugar can be the cause of metabolic diseases, lack of concentration and confusion. Babies and toddlers who go sugar-free are usually much more balanced and much calmer and become more rarely ill than children who consume a lot of sugar. Meanwhile, research suggests that not only protein deposits from meat, egg and milk consumption, but also excessive sugar consumption in the last 200 years may be a cause (or perhaps the cause) of senile dementia and Alzheimer's disease. These diseases are now also

known as brain diabetes. In traditional Chinese medicine, the pancreas is a part of the spleen which controls the ability to relate and handle relationships. For this reason, excessive sugar consumption can also be the cause of disharmonies and imbalances in relationships. More and more research results indicate that the **most common (everyman's) drugs** include the following food components: agglutinins, gluten, yeast, animal products and sugar.

Are humans designed for meat digestion?

Humans have grinders. Beings with grinders do not eat meat in the biorhythmic ecological balance and in peace and harmony within themselves, as well as between themselves and all beings and life itself. For the maintenance and restoration of the biorhythmic ecological balance in a comprehensively healthy growth and in the flow of being and living which nourishes the power of light and love and where, in all energy flows, exclusively love flows freely in a closed cycle, there are special animal species in the animal world with fangs and/or claws or talons for catching prey.

For digestion, humans enter into a symbiosis with microorganisms, which amount to 1.5 to 2 kg of their body weight. The digestive symbiosis in humans is overburdened with the digestion of animal products (also with casein, which is a special protein for calves, in milk). In addition, the intestines in humans are much too long for the digestion of meat, which needs a very short intestine. When people eat meat, undigested meat remnants remain in the intestines. Fungi, lactic acid bacteria and photosynthetic bacteria then attack the dead matter in the intestine and decompose undigested matter **in a decay process** in the intestine. This creates toxins in the intestine with toxic decay gases, which escape outwards through the macerated intestinal wall and get into the bloodstream. The toxins then get into the entire organism via the bloodstream. Due to the acid environment in the intestinal biotopes, the intestines are also a breeding ground for fungi and parasites. Since fungi excrete pure alcohol, the liver, the largest detoxification organ in the body, is stressed and weakened even without alcohol being consumed.

The result is that the acid-base metabolism in the blood becomes more and more disharmonious and imbalanced. Since the blood becomes more and more “acidic”, it is also a breeding ground for fungi and parasites. These uninvited guests get into the entire organism via the blood. Since fungi and parasites devour vast amounts of sugar and carbohydrates, people with a fungal infection or a parasite infestation are constantly tired and lack energy. Fungal infections and parasite infestations are the cause of cravings for sugar and carbohydrates. The externally visible symptoms of fungal infections are nail and skin fungi. According to TCM, the most frequent causes of death are fungi and parasites in the organs (preferably in the lungs). Such diagnoses are not made in orthodox medicine.

When consuming animal food, not only protein is consumed, but also the nature of the animals and all energies, vibrations and emotions from feeding, breeding, animal husbandry, factory farming ... are absorbed. Since the animals are killed against their will, humans are also confronted with the death shock of the animals. Fears, shocks, anxiety attacks and nightmares that have manifested within a person can become even stronger with the consumption of animal products. In adults and children (clients) such symptoms disappeared shortly after switching to an animal-free diet.

The behaviour (social, sexual, dietary, etc. behaviour) of people who repeatedly absorb the nature of animals, their energies, vibrations and emotions, is often no longer identical to that of “the human being”, but becomes more and more similar to the nature of animals.

Energies, vibrations and emotions in fungi

Fungi are the most widely distributed organisms on Earth. Fungi, which are not animals, plants or bacteria, form their own large group of living organisms. Fungi are involved in the decomposition of dead organisms (dead matter). Together with lactic acid bacteria and photosynthetic bacteria, they decompose dead organisms in a decay process back to earth, so that the biorhythmic ecological balance in a comprehensively healthy growth is maintained on our planet. Fungi in the biorhythmic ecological balance only attack diseased or dead organisms in keeping with their mission in life. An acidic environment in the organism (in the intestines and blood) is a breeding ground for fungi and parasites. As soon as there are no more “breeding

grounds" (acidic environment), fungi and parasites leave the organism via the excrements.
The largest living creature in the world is a fungus of the species *Armillaria solidipes*. It grows in America and its mycelium occupies an area of **nine** square kilometres in the underground. In the biorhythmic ecological balance fungi have "power over other organisms" due to their mission in life (decomposing organisms). Furthermore, they are the "largest population group of living beings" on our planet.
People who want to spread extremely and have "power" over other beings obtain power energies from outside, also through their diet (e.g. from mushrooms).
When fermenting soya sauce (shoyu), miso, vegetables and sauerkraut (pickled cabbage), enzymes and bacteria convert the sugar in the food into lactic acid. During a longer fermentation process, lactic acid bacteria are often joined by fungi, which then trigger a "putrefaction process" together with the lactic acid bacteria. This is also the case with yeast and sourdough bakery products (yeast bread, yeast cake and sourdough bread). A dough with many carbohydrates and sugar offers an ideal breeding ground to lactic acid bacteria and yeast fungi. Since lactic acid bacteria and yeast fungi multiply strongly in the dough and begin to decompose the dough in a fermentation process, the dough rises. When the bread or cake is baked, all lactic acid bacteria or yeast fungi (living organisms) die due to the intense heat in the oven; the fermentation process comes to an abrupt end.
When people eat food (yogurt, cheese, bread ...), which was produced with the help of lactic acid bacteria and yeast fungi (living organisms), then they not only absorb energies, vibrations and emotions of the food itself (milk, flour, sugar ...), but also the "nature" and all energies, vibrations and emotions (including the death shock of the mass extinction in the oven) of the living organisms (lactic acid bacteria, yeast fungi) with the help of which the products were produced.

Agglutinins and gluten are extremely harmful to health

Agglutinins and gluten that are present in many cereals, especially in wheat and spelt ... can cause inflammations in the whole organism with often bad effects as a long-term consequence. Instead of agglutinin- and gluten-contaminated cereals, I only include **gluten-free** cereals in my diet, such as millet, rice and buckwheat (a *Persicaria* [knotweed] plant that can be used like cereals).

Agglutinins and gluten cannot be completely broken down into individual amino acids by symbiotically living microorganisms. Undigested gluten fragments and agglutinins are so small that they can pass through the intestinal wall and get into the bloodstream without hindrance. They then dock with healthy cells, preferably immune cells, and trigger inflammations everywhere in the organism, which, in further consequence, can cause serious health damage in the organism. However, these inflammations inside the body are usually not noticed at all. Agglutinins and gluten can emulate endorphins (endogenous substances), which have important functions in the brain, participate in the sensation of pain or happiness and in controlling the feeling of hunger, cloud the senses, create confusion and be the cause of lack of energy and concentration disorders. Many people are addicted to agglutinin- and gluten-containing cereals. This addiction can be compared to the addiction to cocaine. This is why gluten is referred to as the "opium in cereals".

Agglutinins and gluten are often the cause of swelling and inflammation in the intestines with fistulas, which cause a strong and unpleasant sensation of pain. In the brain, the inflammations and swellings caused by agglutinins or gluten are perceived as a "befogged feeling" or as a migraine attack with a strong sensation of pain.

Can gluten sensitivity be the cause of health problems?

In orthodox medicine, coeliac disease is a disease that is diagnosed due to gluten intolerance. However, coeliac disease only occurs in 1 in 100 people, while **agglutinins affect all people equally**. Other health problems are not associated with gluten or agglutinins in orthodox medicine (similarly to milk

and sugar). Although there have been many research findings on the adverse health effects of agglutinins and gluten for a long time, orthodox medicine does not pay any attention to the effects of agglutinins. I found detailed statements to this topic in the book of Dr. Dr. Probst with the title “Warum nur die Natur uns heilen kann” (Why only nature can heal us).
There have been studies over a period of ten years with patients diagnosed with fibromyalgia by orthodox medicine due to unexplained whole-body pain. These studies report that these patients were either pain-free or noticed a significant improvement after only eight weeks after they were on an elimination diet, which means that they avoided not only gluten but also other foods that had turned out to be problematic for them personally in the IgG test.
Other symptoms such as word-finding disorders, back pain, migraine, depression, irritable bladder, painful periods, tingling or numb feet, tinnitus, dry mucous membranes, swollen hands, feet and face etc. have also significantly improved in these test patients.
A study result on the interrelationships and effects of gluten in autistic children was published in the online journal *PLoS One* in June 2013.
Researchers asked themselves, among other things, whether the consumption of gluten leads to autoimmune attacks on the nervous system and came to the conclusion that a gluten-free diet (which is automatically also agglutinin-free) helps autistic children. In a case study, it was found that an autistic child, who also suffered from epilepsy, was seizure-free already after starting a gluten-free diet and even after 14 months (at the time of publication of the case study). As a side effect, the child’s intelligence quotient increased by 70 points. Children who suffer from coeliac disease and **need** a gluten-free diet are usually more receptive and concentrated at school than their classmates. (Information sources: https://www.zentrum-der-gesundheit.de/gluten and the books of Dr. Dr. Probst.)
Only if you get involved in your own nutritional experiences, can you make clear and above all self-convinced nutritional decisions for yourself (decisions based on your own perceptions in self-regeneration and self-healing). Although the studies recommend a 60-day gluten-free diet while excluding other causes of symptoms, a recurring diarrhoea with weight loss was no longer an issue for me after just a few days. My body weight has returned to normal with the gluten-free diet after only a few weeks.

Symptoms (signals) protect against serious diseases and long-term consequences

Disharmonies and imbalances in the body, mind and soul, in relationships, situations and communication draw people's attention to behaviours that are not identical to themselves. These "alarm signals" are important so that people with diarrhoea or flatulence, for example, can change their eating habits. It is particularly difficult for people to let go of their eating habits or addictions because they have often been manifested in family systems for several generations.
Due to (food) intolerances, people also go to see "healers" instead of changing their eating habits. There is a healer living near my hometown who is consulted by many people. Those going to see this woman believe that she can "erase" body reactions such as diarrhoea, flatulence ... due to (food) intolerances in one treatment. The "healer" was a pharmacist and, together with a colleague, spent years researching a treatment method "for erasing body symptoms" in case of intolerances. People who believed in the effect of the treatment for some time indeed did not suffer from flatulence after drinking milk or from unpleasant diarrhoea after drinking beer. However, with distrustful people her treatment was always unsuccessful. Even if symptoms are magicked away, this does not improve blood values, deposits do not disappear and the body weight is not reduced. The opposite is the case, because people who do not have any unpleasant symptoms (alarm signals) are even less willing to change their lifestyle and eating habits, which are the cause of overacidification, deposits, obesity, etc. Due to the persistent adherence to their lifestyle and eating habits, these people continue to be at risk for serious diseases such as stroke, heart attack or cancer and, in the long run, also for Alzheimer's disease and senile dementia. Above all, these people remain long-term customers of the pharmaceutical industry.

Food supplements

There is a battle for market shares for food supplements. Lone warriors, pharmacies and the pharmaceutical industry argue for their products. Even the

best arguments are counterproductive for the ecological balance in a comprehensively healthy growth, as many people then tend to take food supplements before they change their non-organic and non-ecological lifestyle-related, dietary and consumer behaviour. The fatal thing about it is that food supplements can only be produced if the ecological balance with a diversity of plant and insect species on our planet is maintained, since only then are there raw materials (plants, blossoms, seeds, etc.) for the production of such products.
Food supplements made from conventionally grown herbal raw materials that have not been biochemically produced are also contributing to the destruction of the biorhythmic ecological balance on our planet.
If, in spite of an organic, healthy diet, mineral deficiencies are found during blood analyses, then I recommend as a first measure to eat **life and root force-strengthening** organic foods with the required mineral nutrients. In case of severe deficiency symptoms, please only consume **vegan, gluten- and sugar-free, biochemically produced food supplements with an organic certificate**.

In an advertisement for "pre-germinated barley" I found the following statement about the barley powder (food supplement): "Pre-germinated barley is undoubtedly a major breakthrough in food technology. As a result of pre-germination, the barley grain is now activated and ready to produce the barley plant, which is why at this point all enzymes are released to a high degree for production. This biochemical state is then practically frozen."
Industrial processing causes the barley seedlings to die. When a soul has incarnated into a plant seed, it wants to develop—just as humans and animals after incarnation—into a strong and healthy plant after germination, a plant which can produce healthy offspring (in this case cereals). Furthermore, barley is **not an agglutinin- and gluten-free cereal**.
If, instead of a denatured powder, an agglutinin- and gluten-free organic cereal (seed for the offspring) is consumed, which has been grown in the biorhythmic ecological balance and in a comprehensively healthy growth, the organism will be strengthened with many **life and root forces**.
Particularly when changes in life occur, such as a change of residence, change of school, change of job or suddenly being a father/mother, people always need strong **life and root forces**.

If parents make sure that their own life and root forces and those of their children are strengthened **with the right food**, they and their children will always have solid ground beneath their feet when life changes.

Food trends

Many people are looking for a diet that is right for them and are often confused and insecure due to different views and opinions (orthodox medicine, TCM, macrobiotics, mother's and grandmother's kitchen, etc.). In my circle of acquaintances more and more people have a vegetarian or vegan and gluten-free diet.
People are also switching from a conventional diet to an organic diet because they no longer want to be co-responsible for destroying the ecological balance.
In the magazine *Universum*, I found the following article titled "Nachhaltig besser leben" (Living better by living sustainably):
When asked why we should eat less animal products, the nutrition ecologist von Koerber answers: More than a third of the world's grain harvest is fed to animals to produce meat, milk and eggs—in Germany even two thirds. The main problem is: The conversion of plant products, which humans could largely consume directly, into animal products is partly not very effective. To produce one kilogramme of meat, you need many times that amount of grain, which you could also eat directly. About 70–90% of food calories are lost as so-called processing losses—a great waste of raw materials in view of the world's approximately one billion starving people.

The food manufacturing industry and retailers react rapidly to food trends

Retailers offer mock meat (also known as fake or faux meat), an imitation of meat products such as sausages ... using vegan sources. People buy these products because they believe that these meatless imitations are healthier. Seitan, a protein from **agglutinin- and gluten-containing** wheat or spelt, can no longer provide life and root forces due to the processing during production.

For this reason, Seitan, which is contaminated with agglutinins and gluten from wheat or spelt, is not suitable for a life and root force-strengthening diet. Only direct vegetable sources of protein from organic beans, organic lentils and organic chickpeas nourish our body by **strengthening our life and root forces**. (Some) protein is present in almost all foods, also in fruits, vegetables, cereals and nuts. Those who want to live animal-free (vegan) out of conviction do not need "imitations" of meat, dairy and egg products like vegan sausages, vegan butter, etc.
In almost all (finished) products offered by retailers (also in organic finished products) there are additives for a longer shelf life and a better consistency. It is only by carefully reading the contents of finished products that you can protect yourself from substances that **you do not want to ingest**. Organic finished products are out of the question for me as well. I prepare all my dishes myself from unadulterated and organic food.
Vegan cookbooks are offered not only in bookstores, but also in supermarkets due to the trend of vegan nutrition. In these cookbooks there are recipes in which animal products are omitted, but the importance of the origin (organic, regional, seasonal) of the food is not pointed out. Furthermore, I find far too few plant protein sources in the recipes. The superfine flours and the sugar used in the recipes could also cause health problems in the long term.
People who with an otherwise conventional diet only omit killed animals or animal products in general (live conventional vegetarian or vegan lifestyles) and do not draw from the abundance of the seasonal and regional organic offer that is in line with the seasonal **biorhythm**, especially from the abundance of plant organic protein sources, often fail when changing their diet due to deficiency symptoms leading to health problems.
Manufacturing industries and retailers have reacted immediately to this situation and offer many food supplements especially for vegetarians and vegans.

My food sources include ...

... edible herbs and flowers (self-)collected on my organic meadow, (self-)grown organic vegetables, organic fruit, organic nuts, organic chestnuts,

organic legumes and gluten-free organic cereals. I get gluten-free organic cereals, organic beans, organic lentils, organic spices, organic potatoes, organic fruit and organic pumpkin seed oil whenever I need them from a convinced organic farmer. In organic grocery stores I buy organic oils, regional rock salt and organic nuts whenever I need them.
I only eat seeds and fruits in which no souls have yet incarnated. I only use organic waxy potatoes (seeds beneath the ground) as long as they are not yet sprouting. As soon as sprouts appear, these potato seeds are planted in spring. Organically grown herbs, seeds and fruits (organic foods) provide the organism with strong **life and root forces** if they are consumed as naturally as possible. The full grain gently boiled in water is the most natural way to consume cereals. When cooking in water, the water should simmer only slightly so that the food cooked in the element water does not lose its harmonious vibration during cooking. This should also be taken into account when preparing tea; never pour overheated and turbulent water over the tea leaves. You should also avoid preparing food with hot air (here the element metal/air is extremely agitated and overheated) or by steam cooking. In steam cooking, food is prepared "under pressure". If people eat food prepared under pressure, they could go into resonance with energies, vibrations and emotions that increase performance pressure and perfectionism.
In spring until late autumn, before the first frost comes, I find many wild and medicinal herbs on my natural meadow, in which I only cut off the greenery, as I do with the organically grown aromatic and medicinal herbs and leaf lettuces in the garden. This procedure does not destroy plants and plants have the possibility to continue growing in the biorhythmic ecological balance and in a healthy growth and to sprout again. Pumpkins from my garden are a special gift for me. I also have a lot of pleasure with the chayotes, the New Zealand spinach (an old, very abundant variety with vine formation), the sweet fennel, the curly kale (also known as "green cabbage"), the Chinese mallow and the watercress. I only grow plants which I can harvest until frost and which leave their place to the offspring next year through sowing their own seeds or which sprout again in spring after winter. Plants that sprout again in spring include hardy spices, hardy onion, garlic, sweet fennel and curly kale (also known as "green cabbage"), which I can harvest even in winter. My herbs and salads still have a lot of bitter substances within them. Many of these garden gifts can also be grown in clay pots with organic soil on a balcony.

During the winter months I use dried herbs, which I dried seasonally, and fruits, which I preserved without sugar seasonally. Apples, pears, but also chayotes and butternut squashes are very well storable until there are meadow and garden gifts again in spring. In the winter months, I eat a salad with a raw chayote at least once a week, because by doing so my immune system will not break down during the winter months. I harvest Jerusalem artichoke, a seed under the earth, in spring before it sprouts, in late autumn after the mother plants have withered or in winter when the earth has thawed due to foehn winds, directly from the earth. This seed gift provides me with many vital and mineral substances for my health.

5.4. Strengthen your life and root forces with life and root force-strengthening food

Time and again, people who suffer from burnout or from eating and sleeping disorders go to see me. These people have often completely lost touch with living in line with the seasonal **biorhythm**. Outwardly oriented and consumerist people buy to eat what is offered by retailers in a consumerist and profit-oriented way—due to group pressure and as if they were remote-controlled.

If people cook denatured foods contaminated with pesticides, flavour enhancers, preservatives and harmful substances from packaging, irradiation and nitrogen storage, **without life and root forces**, they lose their joy and creativity when preparing their food due to the poor vibration in the food. It is very bad when people, among them athletes and people who exercise regularly, eat denatured, “dead”, powdered (protein) food, which only has to be dissolved in water.

A dietary behaviour that is not identical to oneself, i.e. eating denatured food, is the cause why the genuine, pure and clear sensory perceptions of what is consumed and the pleasure when eating, without addictive behaviour, are more and more lost. A bad consequence of this is that people begin to reject “food” and become anorexic or addicted to (additional) substances in denatured food and scoff health-damaging food without life and root forces as if they were “remote-controlled” and until they become obese.

The cries of the organs can then be seen mainly in the face. In TCM (Traditional Chinese Medicine), a facial diagnosis immediately reveals imbalances and disharmonies in the organs. A lifestyle-related and dietary behaviour that is identical to oneself is reflected in an uninterrupted, independent identity line, which is also referred to as digestive or life line and is separated from relationship lines, around the thenar eminences on the inside of the left and right hand.
Not being able to enjoy food any more, overeating, overacidification, etc. are consequences of a dietary behaviour that is not identical to oneself.
Only with a **regional and seasonal organic diet** that is adapted to the seasonal **biorhythm** and **strengthens the life and root forces** can one (again) achieve a biorhythmic ecological balance and a comprehensively healthy growth.
An organic, life and root force-strengthening, regional and seasonal diet that is in line with the seasonal **biorhythm detoxifies and purifies** the organism, **nourishing** it with strong, direct **life and root forces**. It brings the **acid-base metabolism in the blood** back into harmony and balance.

With a **seasonal and regional, organic, life and root force-strengthening diet** that is in line with the seasonal **biorhythm**, you will feel more comfortable in your stomach and clearer in your mind after just a few days. Unpleasant physical and psychological symptoms often disappear after a short time. Recurring diseases and pains such as back, knee and hip pains, gout knots, skin diseases such as acne, boils and abscesses, fungal infections, metabolic diseases such as diabetes and digestive problems (diarrhoea, constipation, flatulence, abdominal pain, etc.), chronic fatigue, insomnia, panic attacks and depressions, migraine, headaches, arthrosis, arthritis, cysts, growths, allergies, food intolerances, autoimmune diseases, irregular blood pressure, asthma, cholesterol, osteoporosis, menstrual pain, menopausal symptoms, inflammation of the bladder and much more are often no longer an issue after a short time or are healing.

The blood renews itself within 120 days (four months). With alkaline blood, physical and mental illnesses can be cured. After four months of keeping to a life and root force-strengthening organic diet that is in line with the seasonal biorhythm, you will be a new person.

During this time, people are in a strong process of self-purification, self-regeneration and self-healing. They increasingly become aware of personal issues within themselves, as well as between themselves and beings and life itself. After detoxification, purification and cleansing (blood renewal), one feels like a “new person” with the desire to **live out one’s identity and individuality “in the here and now”**. In such a state, one automatically begins to clear out all places (environment, living spaces ...) of being and living as well as all relationships within oneself, as well as between oneself and all beings and life itself, in singledom and coupledom, as well as in professional, business, leisure and social life.
Metabolic waste products, toxins, deposits and excess body weight are completely broken down by the organism during this time. In the case of underweight, the weight returns to the normal weight range.
When following an organic, life and root force-strengthening diet that is in line with the seasonal biorhythm, people experience that **they can heal themselves with food**.

During the 120 days (four months) acid-forming foods, such as meat, eggs, milk, sugar, extremely salty foods and all stimulants and addictive substances such as alcohol, nicotine, coffee ..., and oven-baked bread and cakes made from cereals containing agglutinins and gluten are completely eliminated for the regeneration of the acid-base metabolism in the blood.

5.5. Experiences with my dietary changes

After my first dietary change in 2007, when I omitted animal products (meat, milk, eggs) and sugar, unpleasant recurring symptoms, such as sinusitis and rheumatic pain in joints and muscles, completely disappeared after only a few weeks. After a short time, I no longer felt a craving for sweets due to an addiction to chocolate and sugar. Such nutrition-related symptoms have never occurred since my first dietary change.
My “new way of cooking” was very well accepted in my family from the beginning. In the first year after my dietary change I wanted to buy a halibut for my family before the Christmas holidays. When I was in the supermarket

on my way to the refrigerated fish counter, I suddenly felt sick and dizzy. I had to leave the shop (without fish) immediately. At home I explained to my family that it is neither possible for me to buy animal products nor to prepare animal products. This was accepted by my family and none of my family members wanted to do the cooking themselves. With an animal- and sugar-free diet, we experienced very peaceful Christmas holidays.
Our daughter, who lived with her life partner and her daughter with us at that time, had a vegetarian diet before. During her second pregnancy her energy balance was also very good with this diet and she was able to fully breastfeed her son for more than a year. Her partner also felt that he had more strength and could sleep much better. Serious metabolic diseases, from which my husband had suffered for many years, **completely** disappeared after he had been on an organic, life and root force-strengthening diet that is in line with the seasonal **biorhythm**.
I lived out my enthusiasm and creativity with much joy and gratitude when cooking with seasonal and regional organic ingredients which had been selected according to the seasonal **biorhythm** and thus contained **strong life and root forces**. I invited friends, craftsmen working for us and also hard-working forestry workers for dinner. None of my guests ever refused a life and root force-strengthening dish that I offered. A forestry worker even wanted to take home recipes for his wife because he liked the food so much and because he could do the hard forestry work more harmoniously and with more concentration with this food.
My daughter and her family had already moved out when I changed my diet for the second time, omitting agglutinins and gluten completely. An unpleasant, recurring diarrhoea with weight loss, which made me aware of my gluten sensitivity, disappeared after a short time. My body weight also normalised after a short time. A few weeks after the omission of agglutinins and gluten, adhesions and mucus in the head and intestinal areas dissolved; I excreted them through the nose and stool. Since I have been omitting agglutinins and gluten from my diet, my sensory perceptions, intuition, instinct and mind have become clearer and more comprehensive. I can centre myself and concentrate better with a good far-sightedness, insight and overview. I perceive my limits and the limits in my environment much better and it is much easier for me now to communicate my limits to my environment.

My husband did not react at all to my second dietary change. Although he still eats denatured, non-organic food abroad and on journeys or when invited, the gratitude and pleasure when eating life and root force-strengthening organic food that is in line with the seasonal biorhythm are constantly increasing. If he eats denatured food (while travelling or on the way) over a longer period of time, he will again experience unpleasant metabolic symptoms such as diarrhoea, vomiting, burping, flatulence and general discomfort. I also notice significant changes in his nature, because he then goes into resonance with (self-)blocking and (self-)destructive energies, vibrations and emotions. If the level of suffering is already very high due to unpleasant physical and psychological symptoms, he drinks only alkaline teas for one or two days. He also makes sure that he only eats life and root force-strengthening, organic and basic dishes until he has recovered. I observe again and again that, during this time, he does not only get rid of unpleasant physical symptoms and depressive mood swings, but also reaches a higher level of (self-)awareness, (self-)perception and (self-)knowledge; in addition, his flexibility, calmness, centredness and concentration significantly improve. And what's more, he gets very creative in his handicraft workshop (without any multimedia influences) or with clearing out and renovating the house.

5.6. Detoxification, purification, clear-out and harmonisation of the acid-base metabolism in the blood

Everyone knows the fairy tale of a poor hungry girl who was given a pot by an old and very wise woman, which the girl could make cook millet porridge using her willpower. When the girl said, "Cook, little pot, cook," the pot would cook millet porridge, and when she said, "Stop, little pot", it ceased to cook.
From this fairy tale I deduce that in the time when the fairy tale was written, people ate their fill with gluten-free millet porridge. In macrobiotic cuisine, which is largely in line with TCM (Traditional Chinese Medicine), a warm breakfast is highly recommended. The advantages are obvious from an energetic point of view. At night the digestion rests; it only slowly becomes active again in the morning. A warm soup (buckwheat soup, squash soup, etc.),

buckwheat *Sterz* (traditional rural dish made from cereals) or a warm millet or buckwheat porridge with stewed seasonal fruit is the ideal morning start and a gentle start for the stomach. These dishes are also suitable for evening meals, which should not be eaten after 5 pm, as this allows for undisturbed self-regeneration and self-healing while you deeply relax in deep sleep during the night.

Food preparation

You should not prepare food in a microwave oven, on an induction cooker or in induction cooking pots with a magnetic core—this would expose the food to high-frequency electromagnetic waves and magnetism. I cook with pollutant-free glass pots and a cast-iron pan. The cast-iron pan should never come into contact with water. Also avoid cooking and baking with hot air and steam cooking; with such cooking methods, the food absorbs blocking and destructive energies and vibrations, which are not in line with the vibrations of beings. Such cooking methods are often the cause that people, despite seasonal and regional, life and root force-strengthening organic ingredients in dishes, remain tired and weak or that health problems do not improve.
The healthiest way to prepare warm food is to cook on a wood-fired kitchen stove. Dishes prepared with electricity using an electric stove should be taken from the hotplate or out of the oven; afterwards, the lids should be removed from the cooking pots and the food should be allowed to stand briefly (preferably in the fresh air outdoors, on a balcony or with an open window) so that **electromagnetic** waves can dissipate. If the kitchen is well ventilated during cooking and after cooking, you also have a good indoor climate during eating.
If you have a wood-fired kitchen stove at your disposal, you should prepare all the life and root force-strengthening organic meals on the kitchen stove. Since many people do not (any longer) have access to such a cooking facility, I will describe how to prepare my dishes on an electric stove.
The crockery and utensils used in the kitchen should be free of harmful substances (above all, they should not contain any plasticisers). I removed plastic and plastic utensils, coated pans as well as aluminium foils and

aluminium pots from my kitchen because it was found out that people who "experimentally" drank water contaminated with aluminium over a longer period of time had aluminium deposited in their brains. I use sealable jars as storage cans. There are also drinking bottles made of glass, which are suitable to take away, also for children. My kitchen utensils are made of pollutant-free and untreated natural materials, preferably solid wood, glass or clay. I only use solid wood boards without gluing and instead of electric kitchen machines I use a potato masher, a potato ricer and a mechanical straining machine. I keep dried herbs in organic linen bags so that the herbs can breathe and do not lose their flavours. Food supplies and spices are best stored in a pollutant-free solid wood cabinet.
You should exclusively buy untreated organic food and organic spices, which are offered openly or are packed organically in paper, linen, etc., are free of preservatives, have not been irradiated and have not been stored in nitrogen, and show the EU organic control label (green leaf). I buy organic millet, organic buckwheat, organic lentils, organic beans, organic potatoes, organic pumpkins, organic apples and organic spices directly from a convinced organic farmer. Unfortunately, supermarkets, but also many organic grocery stores mostly offer organic food with the EU organic control label (which states that the organic product comes from an EU-controlled organic farm) that contains preservatives, is sold in packaging contaminated with harmful substances (in plastic) and has been stored in nitrogen. Tetra packaging for liquid food products has an aluminium layer between the cardboard layers. Aluminium contaminants will move from the packaging into the liquid food product. Environmental organisations are campaigning for a legal regulation banning silver ions in packaging used to prolong the shelf life of food products. Silver ions are also incorporated into many sportswear fabrics because they prevent the formation of odours in sweat. Non-organically packaged (organic) foods that have been treated with preservatives and stored in nitrogen are contaminated with harmful substances. This causes raw (organic) foods to lose the natural electrons that are needed in the organism and hold everything together.
I also use fresh and/or dried meadow and garden herbs as iron suppliers and for the good taste in dishes. I use salt sparingly, as salt is also harmful to health if overconsumed. I use the non-iodised, 100% natural (without additives for prolonging the shelf life and without anticaking agents), unrefined regional

rock salt from Bad Aussee. Before I use the sea salt, which is petrified and sheltered inside the mountain and enriched with many minerals, I direct my love towards it. Then I put it in the sun for a few hours. Flooded with my love and the sun, the salt that has been trapped inside the mountain for 150 million years without sun (light) releases depressive, rigid, petrified, inflexible, blocking and destructive energies, vibrations and emotions. After this loving attention the salt vibrates again with the "awareness of the free beingness in the sun-flooded sea".
Iodised salt with additives for better pourability and a longer shelf life is usually offered in retail stores or online. This salt is also packed in plastic and thus choked. Desert salt is out of the question for me, because in the desert there is no comprehensively healthy growth in the biorhythmic ecological balance any more and because I prefer regional salt.

When preparing your food, always choose dishes that are in line with the regional and seasonal **biorhythm** from the recipes—for breakfast and the main meal. Be creative when experimenting and use exclusively agglutinin-, gluten-, yeast-, animal- and sugar-free, seasonal and regional organic food that is in line with the seasonal **biorhythm** during the 120 days.
For dinner, which should not be eaten after 5 pm, you can have leftovers from breakfast or lunch.
If you are on a diet that is identical to yourself and if you are not hungry in the morning, at noon or in the evening, do not eat until you are hungry, because eating when you are not hungry blocks self-purification, self-regeneration, self-transformation and self-healing. In the winter months I generally get along with two meals a day. On hot summer days I eat less and more raw food during my meals.
After the "winter dormancy" the pulse rate increases. This is why not only animals but also humans become more active in spring. In spring, the organism and the microorganisms living in symbiosis in beings automatically adjust to eating more food that is in line with the seasonal **biorhythm** and comes from the regional environment—due to the (higher) energy demand and for replenishing the mineral deposits. Stinging nettles, wild garlic, ground ivy, ground elder, dandelion ... are excellent calcium, iron, selenium ... suppliers, especially in spring. Stinging nettles are also used together with red algae and red clover for organic and vegan calcium and selenium supplements.

In my opinion, hunger and fasting cures are counter-productive in spring, because the mineral deposits are often empty after winter and have to be replenished via a mineral-rich diet that is in line with the seasonal **biorhythm** until the next winter dormancy starts.

Just as important as nutrition is **exercise** (running, hiking, Nordic walking, ski touring, snowshoeing, cycling, etc.). Join a gymnastics or yoga group in your area.

Important notes

If you are allergic to ingredients in the recipes, do not use these ingredients. Food intolerances often resolve after the fourth week of detoxification and purification. If you are allergic to buckwheat, use millet or Seewinkler natural rice (from Seewinkel in Austria) instead of buckwheat.

Before you **begin with "self-healing through nutrition"**, I recommend that you have a blood analysis done so that you know which vital and mineral substances you need to increase through organic nutrition. It is very important that you also have a blood analysis done **after the four months**.

In case of a serious undersupply of mineral depots only take vegan gluten-, yeast- and sugar-free, biochemically produced **organic food supplements with an organic certificate**. The organism can also react allergically to organic food supplements. After I took a vegan organic calcium preparation with spirulina, which is not a plant but a bacterium and which is often mistakenly called "microalga", my body reacted with strong symptoms, such as an extremely dry, burning mouth, swollen tonsils and diarrhoea. I then increasingly supplied my body with calcium via green leafy vegetables (stinging nettles, wild garlic, collard greens ...).

During orthodox medical treatments, please discuss dietary changes with your treating physician. Nutritional decisions always remain the responsibility of the reader.

Alkaline tea blends made of organic medicinal herbs to stimulate self-healing

- Stinging nettles or birch leaves (use fresh herbs in spring, summer and autumn.)
- Fennel seeds, caraway seeds or aniseed; alternately add some herbs such as thyme, coriander, rosemary, basil, oregano, lemon balm, mallow, mint or sage to the fennel seeds, caraway seeds or aniseed—intuitively and according to taste.

Do not overcook. Similar to Bach flower remedies, the seeds and herbs should only stimulate the self-healing powers in the organism during self-regeneration.
Preparation: Put the seeds and selected herbs in a ceramic or glass teapot, pour hot water over the herbs before it boils effervescently, let the tea brew for five minutes, then filter the tea and refine it with pure organic sea buckthorn juice, because sea buckthorn juice provides plenty of vitamin C.
In the first four weeks, add **five drops of organic grapefruit seed extract** (natural antibiotic) to your tea in the morning, at noon and in the evening unless you are taking medication. During the first four weeks, drink three cups of tea every day; afterwards, you can drink as much tea as you like.

Mallow water

Put fresh or dried organic mallow leaves from the common mallow (*Malva sylvestris*) in clean water with a good pH value in the evening and drink the mallow water the next day and during the first four weeks. The mallow dissolves mucus.

Chlorophyll drink for the liver (seasonal, not possible in winter)

Ingredients: one bowl of seasonal garden and meadow herbs, water

Preparation: Put all the herbs with water into a large pot. Bring the herb water to the boil and let it simmer over the lowest heat for about five minutes. Then filter the hot chlorophyll drink and fill it into clean and sealable ¼-litre glasses. Drink one glass every day with a little freshly squeezed lemon juice or sea buckthorn juice, as this also ensures iron absorption. If the chlorophyll drink is stored in the refrigerator, always warm the drink a little. If it is seasonally possible, drink ¼ litre of chlorophyll drink every day **for one week once a month** during the four months of detoxification and purification.

Water

In order to eliminate all toxins and metabolic waste products, as well as cold, from the organism, drink plenty of clean water with a good pH value, which cleanses the organism, while detoxifying and purifying the body—not in sips, but all at once ¼ litre. Drink at least two to four litres of water a day during the first four weeks, such as mallow water, still water and mineral water with a lot of sodium (which regulates the acid-base balance in the body).

Roasted walnuts

To remove the hydrogen cyanide from the nuts, wash the freshly cracked organic walnuts and soak them in water for two hours two to three times and rinse them well each time. Then spread them on a baking tray and dry them at 130 degrees Celsius (top and bottom heat) for 40 minutes until slightly roasted. Place the baking tray outdoors for cooling. Like seasonal organic chestnuts, roasted walnuts are a welcome and very healthy change. Please use only such nuts—also for your baking creations.

What to keep in mind

From personal and my clients' experience I know that the **agglutinin-, gluten-, yeast-, animal- and sugar-free diet** only works if you ingest **many vital and**

mineral substances from seasonal and regional, life and root force-strengthening organic foods that are in line with the seasonal **biorhythm** and eat at least **10 organic walnuts** a day (or other organic nuts, such as skin-free organic almonds), because walnuts are a source of magnesium and provide folic acid, the vitamins B and E, zinc, selenium and potassium. Please avoid peanuts, because peanuts contain agglutinins. In the case of histamine intolerance, you may try out whether nuts are tolerated again from the fifth week onwards. From experience I can report that intolerances often resolve while detoxifying and purifying the body. In addition, nibble organic sunflower or pumpkin seeds "without traces of gluten" when you feel like it. Use **2–3 tablespoons of cold-pressed organic linseed, rapeseed or fruity olive oil** with lots of omega-3 fatty acids for a salad every day or stir the oil into a cooked dish (do not heat it afterwards). For frying and baking with oil (when preparing fried potatoes, pancakes, etc.) there are heat-resistant organic oils such as organic olive oil or organic sunflower oil. If you feel very cold in winter, you can eat a little more cold-pressed organic oil or more nuts.

Sea buckthorn berries and cornelian cherries are particularly strong vitamin C suppliers. When the berries and cherries are ripe at the end of August, I eat some sea buckthorn berries or cornelian cherries every day. I crush ripe sea buckthorn berries in a wood mortar and dress my salads with the juice mush. The excess berries or cherries are used to prepare juice for the winter. In winter, these juices taste particularly good in tea or strongly diluted with water. Salads dressed with sea buckthorn juice (as sour as lemon) have a particularly high vitamin C content.

Vitamin B12 is ingested in a vegan diet through microorganisms found on unwashed plants, fruit and vegetables. As the vitamin B12 supply during the winter is very difficult on a regional basis, I obtain vitamin B12 in winter from the nori alga and, in case of a severe deficiency, also from a vegan, gluten- and sugar-free, biochemically produced food supplement.

Calcium and iron are provided by seasonal and regional green leafy vegetables (stinging nettles, dandelion, ground ivy, ribwort plantain, strawberry leaves, ground elder, wild garlic, curly kale (also known as "green cabbage"), spinach, sweet fennel, leaf lettuces, onion and garlic leaves, chives, etc.—add some freshly squeezed organic lemon juice to the dish as this ensures iron absorption), green vegetables such as peppers and cucumbers, legumes, fruit and also gluten-free cereals.

Dried stinging nettles with seeds are a source of iron for the winter. Cut off the stinging nettles with the ripe seeds in autumn, dry them (hang them upside down in an airy place) and sprinkle the dried and finely crumbled leaves and seeds over ready-to-eat dishes. I use a herbal mixture of dried ground ivy and dried stinging nettles with stinging nettle seeds.

With a regional **mineral water** from the Koralm region with natural carbonic acid, many minerals such as calcium and a lot of **sodium** we not only quench our thirst, but we also bring our acid-base metabolism back into harmony and balance with the sodium in the mineral water.

During the winter I eat untreated **organic Atlantic algae** (macroalgae, no processed algae) from Galicia in Spain in addition to my regional diet, because algae contain many minerals and vitamins and can replace the "summer garden" in winter. The wakame alga provides calcium, potassium, proteins, fibre and a lot of iodine. The dulse alga contains the vitamins A and C, iron, potassium, proteins and fibre. From the nori alga you can get proteins, vitamin A, vitamin B12 and fibre.

I receive vitamin D, which is needed for healthy and strong bones, directly from the sun from the end of March to the end of September by staying naked (without the influences of soaps, creams and sunscreen products) in the open air for at least two hours on sunny days. In winter I also spend a lot of time outdoors every day, either taking long walks or doing winter sports such as cross-country skiing and snowshoeing. During the winter I also obtain solar energy from an extra virgin organic coconut oil, which I apply to my skin once a week in winter. In addition, since I was 63 years old, I have been taking vegan, gluten-, yeast- and sugar-free, biochemically produced vitamin D3 together with vitamin K2 during the winter months.

All beings also need **energetic vitamin D** for a comprehensively healthy growth in the biorhythmic ecological balance. This vitamin D is **loving care** towards oneself, as well as between oneself and all beings and life itself. If parents love their children, set clear limits identically to the love residing within themselves and live identically to the love residing within themselves while preserving their own identity and individuality, their offspring will usually also develop in a comprehensively healthy growth and in the biorhythmic ecological balance.

Selenium is a trace element that is needed in very small amounts only; we need it to break down free radicals from environmental pollution that we have

absorbed and for the function of the thyroid gland. I obtain selenium from nuts I eat every day.
Every day in the morning I apply the **5% Lugol's solution** from a pharmacy to a thigh (3 x 4 cm)—on the one hand to check whether iodine is needed and on the other hand to supply the body with iodine. I don't think that iodine interacts with drugs, because iodine-containing salt is also available. **Nevertheless, if you are taking medication, please ask your family doctor or pharmacist for information.** If the brown spot has disappeared after 24 hours, the iodine has been absorbed through the skin due to an acute iodine deficiency. Repeat this application only until the iodine is no longer absorbed by the skin and a brown spot is still visible after 24 hours. As soon as you feel sick, groggy and weak again, repeat the iodine treatment (check). Iodine for the thyroid function is particularly important when people are exposed to severe environmental pollution.
For joint pain, I take ½ teaspoon of organic, pure and untreated sulphur powder (MSM) dissolved in water. Do not take MSM at the same time as inorganic sulphur for intestinal cleansing. Organic grapefruit seed extract with the vitamins C and E is a natural antibiotic and helps with (fungal) infections. **Since grapefruit seed extract interacts with medication, only take it if you are not taking medication or after you have checked with your pharmacist or family doctor.**
I recommend that people who take dietary supplements or remedies for medical reasons because their mineral deposits are extremely empty or because they want to treat symptoms only take dietary supplements and remedies which are **biochemically produced from organic substances**, are **agglutinin-, gluten-, yeast-, animal- and sugar-free** and are **organically certified**. First and foremost, however, you should make sure that you get all the minerals and vitamins you need for a comprehensively healthy growth from seasonal and regional, life and root force-strengthening, organic foods that are in line with the seasonal **biorhythm**.

5.7. Nutrition plan (natural remedies) for the first four weeks

During the first four weeks, stir **1 tablespoon of organic psyllium husk flakes** into a tea or water together with some sea buckthorn juice or freshly squeezed lemon juice every day in the morning and at noon as a first intake of food, and drink this mixture quickly half an hour before eating. Drink 5 drops of **grapefruit seed extract** three times a day in a glass of water or tea **unless you are taking medication**.

Apply the **5% Lugol's solution** to a thigh (3 x 4 cm) every day **in the morning**—on the one hand to check whether iodine is needed and on the other hand to **supply the body with iodine**. If the brown spot has disappeared the next day (after 24 hours) in the morning, you have absorbed the iodine due to an iodine deficiency. Continue the treatment only until the brown spot is still visible after 24 hours. Then you also have to stop taking the **brown algae powder, which contains a lot of iodine**.

Otherwise, adults take ½ teaspoon (in case of severe poisoning, 1 teaspoon) and children 1 pinch of organic brown algae powder in the first four weeks (longer if necessary) in the morning; this detoxifies the organism from chemical (metal) contamination and even from radioactive contamination (my own experience). Take the algae powder with plenty of sea buckthorn or lemon water.

Only in case of strong organism contamination adults take 1 teaspoon and children ½ teaspoon of inorganic sulphur powder three times a day in the same way as the brown algae powder. **Please do not inhale the sulphur powder or sprinkle it into your eyes and keep it safe from children.**

Only take the inorganic sulphur until the excrements and evaporations (stool, urine, sweat) no longer smell unpleasant. Depending on how heavily the organism is "polluted", this can take up to half a year in the case of severe poisoning, but also only a week or a few days. Detoxification and purification **with this diet** also works without inorganic sulphur if you do not want to take it.

Food intake in the first week, when inorganic sulphur is used to detoxify and repair the intestines

Take the psyllium husk flakes, the grapefruit seed extract and the brown algae powder half an hour before meals and the inorganic sulphur half an hour after meals (as described).
Breakfast:
In winter, prepare a raw vegetable plate with 1 organic avocado, grated organic Jerusalem artichoke tubers or a grated organic chayote, the juice of an organic lemon, 2 tablespoons of cold-pressed organic fruity olive oil and organic nuts. If winter vegetables are no longer available, use 2 organic avocados.
As soon as there are meadow and garden herbs, mince the organic herbs and prepare the raw vegetables with a few boiled organic waxy potatoes (have less carbohydrates) or with ½ cup of boiled organic buckwheat or boiled organic millet. If cucumbers are seasonally available, cucumbers with organic herbs can also be eaten for breakfast.
Lunch:
A soup and/or a main course that is in line with the seasonal **biorhythm** from my book. As an alternative, you can also prepare dishes with Seewinkler natural rice (from Seewinkel in Austria). Organic nuts for dessert.
Dinner: (Not after 5 pm)
In winter prepare leftovers from lunch and in summer prepare a raw vegetable plate with organic lemon, cold-pressed organic oil and nuts.

Eat mindfully, i.e. concentrate on eating only, taking small bites and chewing them for a long time before swallowing, with all-embracing gratitude and **without external multimedia influences**, such as daily newspapers, radio, TV and mobile phones.

Between meals: As described at the beginning, drink a lot during the first four weeks.

After the first four weeks (without sulphur, from the first week), choose dishes that are in line with the seasonal **biorhythm** from the abundance of recipes—for breakfast and the main meal.

This is what you need for detoxification, cleansing and repair (including inorganic sulphur) in consideration of macrobiotics

- "Sulfur depuratum" (purified inorganic sulphur powder) and, if necessary, organic natural sulphur (MSM)
- 5% Lugol's solution (iodine with potassium iodide) for application to the skin. I obtain the solution from my family doctor.
- Biochemically produced, vegan, organic vitamin D3 (2.500 I. U. per drop) with vitamin K2, if a D3 deficiency was diagnosed
- Organic grapefruit seed extract, organically certified brown algae powder (*Ascophyllum nodosum*), organic psyllium husk flakes
- Organic sea buckthorn juice, sodium-rich mineral water, organic lemons or organic limes
- Organic avocados, organic nuts
- Cold-pressed organic fruity olive oil, cold-pressed organic rapeseed oil and heat-resistant organic olive oil
- Organic spices such as fennel, caraway, coriander seeds, thyme, wild garlic, lovage, marjoram, bay leaves, savoury, basil, oregano ...
- Organic buckwheat, organic millet "without traces of gluten"
- Regional and seasonal organic fresh garden and meadow herbs, organic cucumbers, organic waxy potatoes, organic squashes and pumpkins, organic Jerusalem artichokes ...
- **And a week's holiday without external digital and multimedia influences**

Harvest on natural meadows, in the forest (wild garlic) and in your own organic garden. Buy organic food directly from the organic farmer or preferably in organic grocery stores.

Recommended books: “Warum nur die Natur uns heilen kann” (Why only nature can heal us) and “Der natürliche Weg zu Heilung und Gesundheit” (The natural way to healing and health) from Dr. med. Dr. Karl J. Probst.

5.7.1. **Seasonal and regional life and root force-strengthening dishes that are in line with the seasonal biorhythm**

All dishes are agglutinin-, gluten-, yeast-, animal- and sugar-free.

Quantity information:
1 cup corresponds to ¼ litre. The food quantities are enough for two persons, a big hunger, unexpected guests or even dinner.

Breakfast dishes

Squash soup:
Preparation: see “Main meals” below “Soups”.

Buckwheat soup:
Preparation: see “Main meals” below “Soups”.

Buckwheat or millet with fruit:
Ingredients: ½ cup of organic buckwheat (whole grains) or ½ cup of organic millet, 1 ½ cups of water, 3 organic apples or organic pears (both possible), 1–2 tablespoons of cold-pressed organic oil, seasonal berries, some roasted organic walnuts
Preparation: Pour the buckwheat or millet into a sieve, rinse it thoroughly in the sink and bring it to the boil with the water, then steam the buckwheat or millet over the lowest heat for 10 minutes until soft, turn off the heat and allow the porridge to swell for another 10 minutes. Wash the apples or pears, core them, cut them into small pieces and stew them with a little water until soft.

Then mix the fruit with the buckwheat or millet porridge and briefly place the fruit porridge (without lid) outside so that electromagnetic rays can dissipate from the food. Mix the cold-pressed oil with the fruit porridge, sprinkle some raw seasonal berries over the porridge if you like and eat it as a warm breakfast with some roasted walnuts. Leftovers can also be eaten cold and taken along for a snack on the go.
Since apples and pears not stored in nitrogen are no longer available from March onwards, mix apple and pear sauce or preserved stewed apples, pears or berries with the buckwheat or millet porridge. Recipes for preserving fruits in line with the regional and seasonal biorhythm can be found among the dessert recipes.

Power pudding:

Ingredients: 1 cup of organic millet, 3 cups of water, 5 organic apples or organic pears (both possible), for babies from the fourth month 1 tablespoon and for adults 2 tablespoons of cold-pressed organic rapeseed or organic linseed oil; optionally some freshly roasted organic walnuts and seasonal berries

Preparation: Pour the millet into a sieve and rinse vigorously with water under the tap. Bring the millet to the boil with water and let it simmer over the lowest heat for 15 minutes in the covered pot (stir once in a while), switch off the power and steam the millet porridge on the hot plate for another 10 minutes. Core the apples and/or pears, but leave the peel on them, cut them into small pieces and then stew them with a little water until soft. For babies and people with swallowing problems, drive the apples and/or pears through a straining machine so that coarse fibres can be removed. Add the millet and the organic oil (in the case of babies from the fourth month onwards) to the apple and pear sauce and stir the millet and fruit sauce until creamy with a wooden spoon. Refine the power pudding with fresh berries in summer and serve it with some roasted walnuts. To have a good supply of this dish, fill the power pudding into screw cap jars while it is still hot, allow it to cool and store it in the refrigerator. Always warm the millet pudding from the refrigerator before eating. This life and root force-strengthening "healing food" strengthens babies, children of all ages and the elderly and can be used as a healing food in the case of illnesses. This pudding is also a coveted dessert. At times when

there is no fresh fruit, you can also use organic apple or organic pear sauce preserved without sugar.
The millet porridge base (without fruit) is also excellent for preparing porridge for babies, the elderly and people with swallowing problems adding seasonal vegetables and legumes.

Buckwheat *Sterz* (traditional rural dish made from cereals):
Ingredients: 1 cup of organic wholemeal buckwheat flour without traces of gluten, 2 cups of water, ¼ tablespoon of natural rock salt, 2 tablespoons of cold-pressed organic rapeseed oil or heat-resistant organic sunflower oil
Preparation: Heat the water with the salt to the boiling point, gradually add the buckwheat flour and stir with a wooden spoon until a lump forms. Steam the *Sterz* over the lowest heat for 5 minutes, then turn off the heat and allow the *Sterz* to swell for another 10 minutes on the still hot plate. Remove the *Sterz* from the heat and stir in the cold-pressed oil or fry the *Sterz* in a pan with plenty of heat-resistant organic oil until crispy. During the wild garlic season and at times when fresh garden herbs are available, I put fresh, finely chopped wild garlic or fresh, finely chopped aromatic herbs in the pan.

Oleaginous fruit bread with wild garlic, onion leaves or chives:
Ingredients: 2 pieces of oleaginous fruit bread, wild garlic (optionally with small stinging nettle tips), onion leaves and/or chives, some juice of an organic lemon, a pinch of salt, 2 tablespoons of cold-pressed organic fruity olive oil
Preparation: Put the herbs and the other ingredients in a solid wood mortar, crush them and generously spread them on the bread. Drink organic lemon and herbal tea with the vitamin-rich bread breakfast.

Main meals

Soups

Squash soup:
Ingredients: 1 organic red kuri squash, organic spices: ¼ teaspoon of lovage, parsley, marjoram or oregano, savoury, ground or grated coriander seeds, wild

garlic (as long as fresh herbs are available, use fresh soup herbs, fresh basil and chives for the soup), ½ tablespoon of natural rock salt, water (quantity depending on the size of the quash)
Preparation: Hollow out the squash, but leave the skin on it, cut it into small pieces and bring it to the boil in a stockpot together with all ingredients except the fresh herbs, then turn down to the lowest heat and let the soup simmer lightly for about 10 minutes. Add the fresh herbs to the soup and mash the squash in the soup with a potato masher a bit so that the soup gets a thicker consistency. As a creamy alternative, drive the soup through a straining machine and stir it with a wooden spoon. Squash soup with millet: Add some steamed organic millet to the soup; it tastes good and is more filling. Millet preparation: Rinse 1 cup of organic millet vigorously with hot water. Bring the washed millet to the boil with 2 ½ cups of water, let it simmer lightly for 10 minutes, switch off the hotplate and allow the millet to swell for another 10 minutes on the still hot plate.
For detoxifying and purifying, eat squash and pumpkin dishes at least once a day during the squash season. Squashes and millet have natural “sweetness”, stop cravings for sweets and harmonise the subtle and gross bodies (organism), mind and soul due to their harmonious and earthy vibration.

Buckwheat soup:
Ingredients: ½ cup of organic buckwheat (whole grains), 3 organic potatoes cut into small cubes and/or seasonal vegetables (squash, pumpkin, chayote, courgette, Jerusalem artichoke, green beans, peas), ½ tablespoon of natural rock salt, ¼ teaspoon of ground or grated organic coriander seeds and organic caraway, organic herbs such as lovage, parsley, celery leaves, garlic and onion leaves, basil and chives, 2 litres of water
Preparation: Pour the buckwheat into a sieve, rinse it thoroughly and boil it with the potato cubes and/or the chopped vegetables from the garden, the natural rock salt and the spices for about 15 minutes until soft. With fresh, finely chopped chives, parsley and basil, the soup is a culinary delight and is easily digestible for the stomach and intestines. For a main meal you can add leftovers of boiled beans or lentils to the soup.

Kidney-strengthening bean soup:

Ingredients: 1 cup of organic beans, 2 large or 4 small organic potatoes and/or 1 piece of organic squash or pumpkin, 2 organic tomatoes, 2 bay leaves, ¼ teaspoon of each of the following organic spices: caraway, savoury, marjoram, ground or grated coriander seeds and wild garlic spice, optionally a tiny bit of chilli, ½ tablespoon of natural rock salt, fresh soup herbs, fresh onion and garlic leaves instead of dry wild garlic spice, water, 1 tablespoon of cold-pressed organic oil

Preparation: Wash the beans and leave them to soak overnight; strain the soaking water in the morning and use it to water the flowers. Rinse the beans vigorously with hot water under the sink, bring them to the boil with the spices and water, but without salt in the covered pot and boil them over the lowest heat for about 1 ½ hours until soft. Peel the potatoes and/or the pumpkin/squash piece (do not peel red kuri squashes) and cut them into small cubes together with the tomatoes. Steam the potato/pumpkin/squash and the tomato cubes with a little water and a little natural rock salt until firm to the bite. Add the natural rock salt as well as the steamed potato/pumpkin/squash/tomato cubes to the bean soup and optionally spice up the soup with a pinch of chilli. Sprinkle any fresh soup herbs into the soup and stir in 1 tablespoon of cold-pressed organic oil. The bean soup can also be prepared without vegetables.

Jerusalem artichoke soup:

Ingredients: ½ kg of organic Jerusalem artichoke tubers, 5 organic potatoes, 2 litres of water, ¼ teaspoon of each of the following (or other) organic spices: caraway, marjoram, wild garlic, basil or oregano, savoury, ground or grated coriander seeds; fresh herbs such as lovage, parsley, celery leaves, onion and garlic leaves, ½ tablespoon of natural rock salt

Preparation: Put water, the Jerusalem artichoke tubers (which have been washed with a brush and diced), the potatoes (which have been peeled and diced), salt and all dried spices into a stockpot. Bring the soup to the boil and let it simmer over the lowest heat for 10 minutes in the covered stockpot. To give the soup a thicker consistency, remove the bay leaves, press 2 ladles of soup through the potato ricer and add them back to the soup, and then stir vigorously with a wooden spoon. For children and the elderly, the soup can also be driven through a mechanical straining machine and then stirred until creamy with a wooden spoon. Finally, add fresh, finely chopped herbs to the soup. If you add some steamed buckwheat or millet to the soup, the soup is more filling. The Jerusalem artichoke melts love handles.

Meadow herbs soup:

Ingredients: 3 cups of young stinging nettle tips, 1 cup of dandelion, 1 cup of widow flower (*Knautia*) leaves, some ribwort plantain leaves, a little ground elder, some strawberry leaves, common daisies and ground ivy (many of these herbs can also be found in autumn); ¼ teaspoon of each of the following (or other) organic spices: savoury, ground or grated coriander seeds, oregano and basil (use fresh herbs if possible); some freshly ground or grated nutmeg; garden herbs such as the leaves of hardy onions and garlic, parsley, lovage and celery leaves; 4 organic potatoes, 2 litres of water, ½ tablespoon of natural rock salt, 1 tablespoon of buckwheat or millet flour

Preparation: Wash the meadow herbs and bring them to the boil together with the potatoes (which have been peeled and cut into small cubes) and all spices. Let them simmer over the lowest heat for 5 to 10 minutes. Blend 1 tablespoon of buckwheat or millet flour to a smooth paste with a little water, add the paste to the soup and let the soup thicken. Afterwards, drive the soup through a food mill (mechanical straining machine), so that coarse fibres can be removed. Serve the soup with finely chopped fresh chives.

Asparagus soup:

Ingredients: 1 bunch of organic green asparagus, 2 organic potatoes, fresh organic soup herbs such as lovage, garlic and Welsh onion leaves, parsley, basil and savoury, ½ tablespoon of natural rock salt, 2 litres of water, 1 teaspoon of cold-pressed organic oil

Preparation: Peel the asparagus from the middle to the end with a potato peeler and cut it into small pieces. Bring the asparagus to the boil in a stockpot together with all ingredients except the fresh herbs and boil it over the lowest heat for 10 minutes until soft. Afterwards, add the fresh, finely chopped herbs to the soup. The asparagus soup can also be offered as a creamy soup by driving it through a straining machine.

Tomato soup:

Ingredients: 1 kg of ripe organic tomatoes or 1 litre of preserved tomatoes from the previous year, 1 litre of water, only a tiny bit of chilli and clove powder, ¼ teaspoon of each of the following (or other) organic spices: savoury, finely ground or grated coriander seeds, oregano and lovage (use fresh soup herbs and the leaves of hardy garlic and onions in summer), ½ tablespoon of natural rock salt, 1 teaspoon of cold-pressed organic oil

Preparation: Bring the diced tomatoes to the boil in a stockpot together with all spices except the fresh herbs and let the soup simmer over the lowest heat for 5 to 10 minutes. Add the fresh, finely chopped herbs to the ready-to-eat soup. For a change, you may offer the soup in a puréed form (by driving it through a straining machine). In natural cooking, you consciously do without electrically operated kitchen machines.

Lentil soup:

Ingredients: 1 cup of leftovers of steamed organic lentils, 5 organic potatoes (which have been peeled and cut into small cubes) and/or 1 cup of organic squash or pumpkin (which has been cut into small cubes), ½ teaspoon of each of the following (or other) organic spices: lovage, marjoram, savoury, caraway and ground or grated coriander seeds, 1 bay leave, 2 litres of water, ½ tablespoon of natural rock salt

Preparation: Put the potatoes, the squash/pumpkin, the water and all spices except the fresh herbs into a stockpot and bring them to the boil. Steam them over the lowest heat for 10 minutes until soft. Afterwards, add the separately steamed lentils and all fresh herbs to the soup and stir until well-blended. Such soups can also be prepared with leftovers of beans. If no potatoes or squashes/pumpkins are available seasonally and regionally, prepare the soup without vegetables. In this case, you may add ¼ litre of preserved tomato pieces from the previous year to the soup.

Steamed lentils: Rinse 1 cup of lentils vigorously with hot water under the sink, bring it to the boil in a pot together with plenty of water, 1 piece of wakame alga, 2 bay leaves, ½ teaspoon of coriander seeds, caraway, marjoram and savoury and steam it over the lowest heat for about 1 hour until soft.

Potato soup:

Ingredients: ½ kg of organic waxy potatoes, 2 litres of water; ½ teaspoon of each of the following (or other) organic spices: caraway, lovage, savoury, marjoram, finely ground or grated coriander seeds and wild garlic; 2 bay leaves; use fresh garden herbs such as parsley, basil, onion and garlic leaves and chives in summer; ½ tablespoon of natural rock salt

Preparation: Peel the potatoes, cut them into small cubes, bring them to the boil in a stockpot together with all ingredients and boil them over the lowest heat until soft. Press 1 ladle of the soft-boiled potato cubes through the potato ricer and stir it into the soup (the soup will be creamier). Sprinkle fresh, finely chopped garden herbs over the soup.

Main courses

Millet pans:

Ingredients: 1 cup of organic millet, 2 cups of water; 1 organic courgette or chayote, ½ organic red kuri squash or butternut squash, organic garden herbs such as parsley, some lovage, savoury, marjoram, oregano, basil, the leaves of hardy onions and garlic (use dried wild garlic and other dried herbs in winter), ¼ tablespoon of natural rock salt, 2 tablespoons of cold-pressed organic oil

Preparation: Rinse the millet vigorously with hot water and steam it as usual. Cut the courgette or chayote (peel it gently) as well as the hollowed red kuri squash (unpeeled) or the peeled and hollowed butternut squash into small pieces. Steam the squashes (vegetables) in a covered pot with some water and together with the finely chopped onion and garlic leaves and all spices over the lowest heat for about 5 minutes until firm to the bite. Afterwards, add all fresh, finely chopped herbs to the steamed squashes, mix the millet with the squashes and stir in the cold-pressed oil.

Always prepare millet pans with regional and seasonal vegetables. E.g. in the asparagus season, prepare the millet risotto with a bunch of organic green or white asparagus (peeled and cut into pieces). Make use of the asparagus season in your region, as asparagus dehydrates and detoxifies the organism and stimulates digestion.

Lentil, bean or chickpea stew:

Ingredients: 1 cup of regional organic lentils, beans or chickpeas, 3 cups of water, 1 piece of wakame alga (2 cm x 2 cm), 2 bay leaves, ½ teaspoon of organic spices such as caraway, marjoram, oregano, finely ground or grated coriander seeds and savoury(, use ½ teaspoon of sodium bicarbonate for beans and chickpeas, sodium bicarbonate dissolves acids, legumes soften much faster with sodium bicarbonate); ½ organic butternut squash, 1 small organic red kuri squash, 1 small organic courgette, 1 organic chayote or 4 organic waxy potatoes, the leaves of hardy onions and garlic or wild garlic (spice), ¼ tablespoon of natural rock salt, 2 tablespoons of cold-pressed organic rapeseed oil

Preparation: Leave the beans or chickpeas to soak overnight, strain the soaking water in the morning and use it to water the flowers, lentils do not need to be soaked overnight. Rinse the lentils, beans or chickpeas vigorously with hot water. Cover the lentils, beans or chickpeas with water in a cooking pot and bring them to the boil together with all spices, but without salt. (Use some sodium bicarbonate for beans and chickpeas.) Steam the legumes over the lowest heat for 1–2 hours until soft. Steam the squashes (vegetables) (which have been cut into small cubes) in a pot with some water and salt and together with the finely chopped onion and garlic leaves or the fresh wild garlic for 5 minutes until firm to the bite. Mix the lentils, beans or chickpeas with the steamed squashes and stir in the cold-pressed oil. Always prepare stews with regional and seasonal vegetables. If regional and seasonal vegetables are no longer available according to the seasonal biorhythm, add potato cubes boiled in salted water or preserved tomato pieces to the stew. Legume stews with spices and salt taste good even without vegetables.

Buckwheat *Sterz* dumplings (*Sterz* = traditional rural dish made from cereals):

Ingredients: 1 cup of organic wholemeal buckwheat flour without traces of gluten, 2 cups of water, ¼ tablespoon of natural rock salt for the *Sterz*; ¼ teaspoon of organic spices such as caraway, wild garlic, basil, parsley and oregano (use fresh herbs of the season), heat-resistant organic sunflower or olive oil

Preparation: Prepare a buckwheat *Sterz* as described below "Breakfast dishes". Place the *Sterz* into a bowl and leave it to cool a bit. Either form small balls without herbs with your wet hands or knead fresh, finely chopped herbs and spices into the *Sterz* and then form small balls. Fry the balls in a pan with oil until crispy (toss the balls in the oil in the pan a few times). If you prepared the balls without herbs, sprinkle herbs such as parsley or wild garlic over the fried balls. With a bowl of fresh salad or as a side dish (in combination with asparagus, leafy vegetables, lentils or beans) buckwheat dumplings are a welcome change.

Buckwheat flour pancakes:

Ingredients: 2 cups of water, ½ cup of organic wholemeal buckwheat flour without traces of gluten, some natural rock salt; various organic herbs of the season such as wild garlic, parsley, oregano, basil, onion and garlic leaves; as a variant of the season, the blossoms of 5 elder umbels; heat-resistant organic sunflower or coconut oil

Preparation: Put the buckwheat flour and the salt into a bowl and blend them to a smooth paste with the water using a wooden spoon. Stir all finely chopped aromatic herbs or elder blossoms into the dough. Heat the oil in a pan and put 1 ladle of dough into the pan. Allow the dough to spread by tilting the pan slightly in all directions. Flip the pancake over after 2 minutes. Serve the pancakes together with a bowl of salad or fill them with steamed spinach leaves. Elder blossom pancakes go well with apple sauce. My grandchildren love the pancakes without herbs, either coated with a homemade, sugar-free jam or filled with steamed spinach leaves.

Meadow herb purée:

Ingredients: Meadow herbs such as tender stinging nettle tips, dandelion (use the inner, tender leaves in autumn), wild strawberry leaves, ground ivy, ground elder ..., in summer and in autumn you can also add 1 bowl of New Zealand spinach from the garden, some mallow leaves, some curly kale (also known as "green cabbage") leaves and the leaves of hardy garlic, organic spices such as lovage, savoury, marjoram and some freshly ground or grated nutmeg, ¼ tablespoon of natural rock salt, 2 tablespoons of organic wholemeal buckwheat or millet flour, 2 tablespoons of virgin organic rapeseed oil

Preparation: Wash the meadow herbs and, if available, the garden herbs and steam them in a pot with a tiny bit of water and together with all spices for about 5 minutes until soft. Blend 2 tablespoons of wholemeal buckwheat flour to a smooth paste with water, add the paste to the steamed leafy vegetables and let the mixture thicken. Afterwards, drive the mixture through a food mill (mechanical straining machine), so that coarse fibres can be removed from the herbs. Stir the cold-pressed organic oil and some dashes of lemon juice (for the absorption of iron) into the purèed mixture und do not heat it afterwards. Buckwheat dumplings, Seewinkler natural rice (from Seewinkel in Austria) or steamed organic millet can be served as a side dish to this healthy and tasty meadow herb purée. In autumn I love the seasonal and regional "new potatoes" as a side dish to the meadow herb purée. In summer and autumn, when I have enough garden spinach, I prepare the purée only with garden spinach and the same spices.

Steamed leafy vegetables (chard or New Zealand spinach, stinging nettles and wild garlic):

Ingredients: 1 big bowl of stinging nettle tips (also together with other meadow herbs), organic wild garlic, organic chard leaves or organic New Zealand spinach, organic garden spices such as lovage, parsley, savoury, oregano, basil, garlic and onion leaves or wild garlic spice, some freshly ground or grated nutmeg, ¼ tablespoon of natural rock salt, 2 tablespoons of organic buckwheat or millet flour, 2 tablespoons of cold-pressed organic sunflower oil, some lemon juice from an organic lemon

Preparation: Steam the stinging nettles (and optionally other meadow herbs), the wild garlic, the chard or New Zealand spinach in a pot with a tiny bit of water and together with the aromatic herbs, the ground or grated nutmeg and the natural rock salt. Blend 2 tablespoons of buckwheat flour to a smooth paste with some water, add the paste to the steamed herbs and let the mixture thicken. Before serving, stir the cold-pressed oil and some dashes of lemon juice into the leafy vegetables. These green mineral suppliers go will with side dishes such as buckwheat dumplings, buckwheat *Sterz* (traditional rural dish made from cereals), steamed millet, Seewinkler natural rice (from Seewinkel in Austria) or potatoes.

Steamed curly kale (also known as "green cabbage"):

Ingredients: 1 big bowl of organic curly kale (also known as "green cabbage"), organic garden herbs such as lovage, parsley and garlic and onion leaves, caraway, savoury, a tiny bit of chilli, ½ teaspoon of finely ground or grated coriander seeds, ¼ tablespoon of natural rock salt and 2 tablespoons of cold-pressed organic rapeseed oil

Preparation: Prepared in the same way and served with the same side dishes as the steamed leafy vegetables (chard or New Zealand spinach, stinging nettles and wild garlic).

Steamed leafy vegetables (chard or New Zealand spinach, stinging nettles and wild garlic) on buckwheat *Sterz* (traditional rural dish made from cereals):

Ingredients: Buckwheat *Sterz* prepared with 1 cup of organic buckwheat flour; steamed leafy vegetables (chard or New Zealand spinach, stinging nettles and wild garlic), steam the herbs as described above, but only very briefly, until they wilt; 2 tablespoons of heat-resistant organic rapeseed oil, heat-resistant organic oil for the baking tray

Preparation: Stir 2 tablespoons of oil into the buckwheat *Sterz* and put 2/3 of the *Sterz* on a baking tray greased with oil. Smooth this *Sterz* down with your wet hands until it is about 1 cm thick and spread the steamed leafy vegetables over it. Flatten small *Sterz* portions with your wet hands until they are 1 cm thick, place them on the leafy vegetables and press them down lightly. Bake the leafy vegetables on *Sterz* in the preheated oven at 200 degrees Celsius for about 30 to 40 minutes. Cut the dish into small portions and serve them together with a bowl of fresh salad. Leftovers are coveted snacks for between meals and can also be eaten cold.

Steamed asparagus:

Ingredients: 1 bunch of organic asparagus, 1 teaspoon of natural rock salt, 2 tablespoons of cold-pressed organic rapeseed oil, fresh organic herbs

Preparation: For 1 portion, peel 1 bunch of organic asparagus, plunge it into boiling salted water, turn the heat down and steam the asparagus over the lowest heat for about 10 minutes until firm to the bite. Strain the soaking water, drizzle the delicious asparagus with virgin organic oil and sprinkle fresh herbs over it. Use the cold asparagus water for dressing salads. Offer seasonal and regional asparagus as a vegetable side dish. Asparagus goes well with the following main courses: steamed millet, buckwheat *Sterz* dumplings (Sterz = traditional rural dish made from cereals), Seewinkler natural rice (from Seewinkel in Austria) and potatoes.

Millet or buckwheat patties in many variations:

Ingredients: 1 cup of steamed organic millet or buckwheat, 1–2 tablespoons of organic buckwheat flour without traces of gluten; 10 wild garlic leaves (for further variations: finely chopped meadow and garden herbs according to taste, such as 1 cup of New Zealand spinach, mallow leaves, ground ivy ..., coarsely grated squash or pumpkin or 1 large grated potato), the leaves of hardy onions and garlic, ½ teaspoon of organic spices, such as wild garlic, marjoram, oregano, basil and parsley (use fresh herbs in summer), some freshly ground or grated organic nutmeg, ¼ tablespoon of natural rock salt, ½ teaspoon of caraway and fennel, heat-resistant organic olive or sunflower oil for frying and baking

Preparation: Place the steamed millet or buckwheat, the wholemeal buckwheat and millet flour, all finely chopped aromatic herbs and the finely chopped wild garlic leaves (meadow and garden herbs of your choice, grated squash/pumpkin or grated raw potatoes) as well as ¼ tablespoon of natural rock salt into a large bowl. Knead the dough vigorously by hand until patties can be formed. Fry the patties briefly in oil on both sides in a pan until golden yellow or place them on a greased baking tray and bake them in the preheated oven at 200 degrees Celsius for about 30 minutes (flip them once). The patties can be served with parsley potatoes, steamed asparagus, steamed curly kale (also known as "green cabbage"), steamed New Zealand spinach, steamed chard, steamed wild garlic, steamed squashes, tomato sauce, fresh salads, etc. Millet and buckwheat patties still taste good when they are cold and are ideal to take with you when you are out and about. Children also like to take them to kindergarten or school as a snack.

Tomato sauce:

Ingredients: 1 kg of very ripe organic tomatoes (in winter: tomato pieces from a jar preserved in the previous year), a tiny bit of water, ½ teaspoon of organic spices such as savoury, marjoram, finely ground or grated coriander seeds, lovage, parsley, onion and garlic leaves or wild garlic, basil (use fresh herbs in summer), a tiny bit of chilli and clove powder, ¼ tablespoon of natural rock salt, 1 tablespoon of organic wholemeal buckwheat flour, 2 tablespoons of cold-pressed organic fruity olive oil

Preparation: Bring the tomatoes (which have been cut into small cubes) and all spices to the boil with a tiny bit of water and steam them over the lowest heat for 5 minutes. Blend 1–2 tablespoons of wholemeal buckwheat flour to a smooth paste with water, add the paste to the tomato sauce and let the mixture thicken. As a creamier variation, drive the tomato sauce through a straining machine, add the cold-pressed oil to the sauce and stir it until creamy with a wooden spoon.

Steamed grated squash or pumpkin:

Ingredients: 1 organic squash or pumpkin, 2 organic tomatoes, onion and garlic leaves (use dried wild garlic spice in winter), ½ teaspoon of organic caraway, 1 tablespoon of organic paprika powder (noble sweet), ½ teaspoon or organic dill, 1 very small pinch of organic chilli, optionally 1 tablespoon of organic buckwheat flour, 2 tablespoons of cold-pressed organic sunflower or rapeseed oil, ¼ tablespoon of natural rock salt

Preparation: Peel and hollow out the squash/pumpkin and coarsely grate the squash/pumpkin pieces with a grater. Steam the squash/pumpkin in a pan with some water and the salt and together with the onion and garlic leaves and all dried spices until soft. Blend 1 tablespoon of buckwheat flour to a smooth paste with cold water, add the paste to the steamed squash/pumpkin and let the mixture thicken. Finally, stir in fresh herbs and the virgin oil. Together with potatoes, millet and buckwheat patties or buckwheat dumplings, the steamed grated squash or pumpkin is a real treat.

Curly kale (also known as "green cabbage") roulades:

Ingredients: 6 large, green organic curly kale (also known as "green cabbage") leaves, ½ cup of steamed organic millet or buckwheat, ½ cup of steamed organic lentils or the leftovers of a lentil or bean stew, onion and garlic leaves or wild garlic, ½ teaspoon of organic spices such as marjoram, savoury, basil or

oregano and parsley, ¼ tablespoon of natural rock salt, heat-resistant organic sunflower or olive oil, ½ litre of soup or tomato sauce diluted with some water
Preparation: Bring water to the boil in a pot. Boil the clean curly kale (also known as "green cabbage") leaves for 3 to 4 minutes. Take the leaves out of the pot and allow them to cool. Place the steamed buckwheat or millet, the steamed lentils or the leftovers of a lentil or bean stew, all spices and the finely chopped onion and garlic leaves or the dried wild garlic spice into a large bowl. Knead a dough. Fill the curly kale (also known as "green cabbage") leaves with a small portion of dough, roll them up and fix the leaves at both ends with a toothpick. Place the roulades into an oven-proof dish greased with heat-resistant oil, pour the soup (e.g. squash soup) or the tomato sauce diluted with some water over the roulades and steam them in the oven for 30 minutes. Take the steamed roulades out of the oven and allow them to stand in the open air before serving them. Curly kale (also known as "green cabbage") roulades go well with regional and seasonal organic waxy potatoes.

Filled bell peppers or courgettes:
Ingredients: 4 bell peppers or 4 small courgettes, the remaining ingredients are the same as for the curly kale (also known as "green cabbage") roulades; tomato sauce diluted with some water or 4 tomatoes (which have been cut into small cubes) and 1 courgette (which has been cut into small cubes), ½ litre of water, ¼ tablespoon of natural rock salt, fresh, finely chopped organic herbs such as parsley, lovage, savoury and basil
Preparation: Cut off the top "covers" of the bell peppers, scrape out the seeds and fill the bell peppers with the dough described above. Put the "covers" back on and proceed in the same way as for the curly kale (also known as "green cabbage") roulades. Cut the courgettes in half lengthwise and scrape out the flesh to make a 1 cm deep shell. Season the scraped-out flesh of the courgettes with wild garlic, steam it briefly in a pan and add it to the dough. The rest of the procedure is the same as for the curly kale (also known as "green cabbage") roulades. Instead of pouring tomato sauce diluted with some water over the filled bell peppers or courgettes, you can put the ingredients described above into an oven-proof dish and place the filled bell peppers or courgettes over the vegetables. Side dishes: fresh salads.

Butternut squash or chayotes baked on a baking tray:

Ingredients: 2 organic chayotes or 1 small organic butternut squash, dried organic wild garlic spice, some natural rock salt, heat-resistant organic oil for the baking tray

Preparation: Peel the chayotes or butternut squash, cut them/it into 1 cm thick slices and sprinkle wild garlic spice and salt over the slices. Place the slices on a baking tray greased with oil. Steam the slices in the preheated oven at 200 degrees Celsius for about 10 to 15 minutes until firm to the bite. Flip them once. A butternut squash or chayotes prepared in this way can be served as a side dish to many meals.

Steamed Jerusalem artichokes:

Ingredients: ½ kg of organic Jerusalem artichoke tubers, organic onion and garlic leaves, ½ teaspoon of organic spices such as caraway, marjoram, basil and savoury, some natural rock salt, heat-resistant organic sunflower or olive oil

Preparation: Clean the Jerusalem artichoke tubers with a brush and cut them into small cubes. Steam the cubes in a pan with some oil and together with the finely chopped onion and garlic leaves and all spices. Steamed Jerusalem artichokes are rich in minerals and go well with the following main courses: waxy potatoes, steamed Seewinkler natural rice (from Seewinkel in Austria) and buckwheat *Sterz* dumplings (Sterz = traditional rural dish made from cereals). Steamed Jerusalem artichokes can be served as a side dish to many meals.

Potato goulash:

Ingredients: ½ kg of organic waxy potatoes, 1 litre of water, ½ tablespoon of natural rock salt, the following organic spices: 1 flat tablespoon of noble sweet paprika powder, 1 very small pinch of chilli, ½ teaspoon of each of the following spices: caraway, savoury, finely ground or grated coriander seeds and marjoram, 2 bay leaves, 2 tablespoons of cold-pressed organic rapeseed oil In winter, I also use 2 tablespoons of a mixture of wakame, nori and duse algae when preparing potato goulash.

Preparation: Wash the potatoes with a vegetable brush under running water, peel them with a potato peeler and cut them into small cubes. Put the water, all spices except the salt and the potato cubes into a cooking pot, heat the water to the boiling point and boil the potato cubes over the lowest heat for 10 minutes until soft. Afterwards, stir in the salt, optionally press 1 ladle of the soft-boiled potato cubes through a potato ricer and stir it into the goulash, remove the cooking pot from the heat and stir in the cold-pressed oil.

Roast potatoes:

Ingredients: 1 kg of organic waxy potatoes, use organic spices such as caraway, marjoram, oregano, rosemary or wild garlic alternately; ¼ tablespoon of natural rock salt, heat-resistant organic oil for the baking tray

Preparation: Peel the potatoes, slice them either crosswise (into slices) or lengthwise (into sticks) and place them into a bowl. Sprinkle the selected spices and the salt over the sliced potatoes and mix everything well. Grease a baking tray with oil and spread the potatoes on the tray. Roast the potatoes in the preheated oven at 200 degrees Celsius (top and bottom heat) for about 35 to 40 minutes. Flip the potatoes after 20 minutes with a spatula. Roast potatoes prepared in the oven of a wood-fired kitchen stove are most palatable. If the roast potatoes are prepared using an electric stove, take them out of the oven and briefly place them outside so that electromagnetic rays can dissipate. Ventilate the kitchen well before serving the roast potatoes.

Herb potatoes:

Ingredients: ½ kg of organic waxy potatoes, organic spices such as rosemary (only) or parsley (only) and/or seasonal herbs from the meadow or garden, the leaves of hardy garlic and onions or wild garlic, some natural rock salt and heat-resistant organic sunflower or olive oil

Preparation: Pour the oil into a frying pan and heat it up very slightly. Put the boiled, peeled and diced potatoes into the pan and sprinkle some rosemary/parsley or seasonal herbs as well as some salt over the potatoes. My grandchildren love it when I mash the potatoes with a potato masher.

Another variation: Allow finely chopped onion and garlic leaves or wild garlic as well as seasonal herbs from the meadow or garden (e.g. garden herbs and ground ivy) to foam up once in some oil, stir in the boiled, peeled and thinly sliced or diced potatoes and salt the mixture with some natural rock salt.

Potato gratin:

Ingredients: ½ kg of organic waxy potatoes, ¼ kg of organic spinach or ¼ kg of organic wild garlic, the leaves of organic hardy garlic and onions (use organic wild garlic spice in winter), organic nutmeg, 1 teaspoon of natural rock salt, heat-resistant organic sunflower or olive oil

Preparation: Boil, peel and thinly slice the potatoes. Put some oil, the finely chopped onion and garlic leaves (or the dried wild garlic spice), the fresh wild garlic or the finely chopped spinach into a frying pan, allow them to foam up once and steam them in the covered pan for 3 minutes. Afterwards, mix the thinly sliced potatoes with the leafy vegetables, salt the mixture with natural rock salt and sprinkle chives and parsley over it.

Boiled potatoes with pumpkin seed oil:

Ingredients: 1 kg of organic waxy potatoes, water, organic pumpkin seed oil, some juice of an organic lemon and some natural rock salt

Preparation: Boil the potatoes in water until soft. Pour the pumpkin seed oil, the lemon juice and the natural rock salt into a small bowl and stir until well-blended. Place the hot, unpeeled potatoes into a large bowl and place it in the middle of the table together with the small bowl with the pumpkin seed oil. During mealtime, the potatoes are peeled on the plate, diced and dipped into the pumpkin seed oil. Even very young children have a lot of fun and feel a success when eating independently in the circle of their family.

Potato pancakes, prepared with boiled potatoes:

Ingredients: ½ kg of organic waxy potatoes that have been boiled, peeled and pressed through a potato ricer, ½ cup of steamed organic buckwheat, 1–2 tablespoons of organic buckwheat flour, ground or grated organic nutmeg, organic marjoram and some organic caraway, organic onion and garlic leaves (use organic wild garlic spice in winter), ¼ tablespoon of natural rock salt, heat-resistant organic olive or sunflower oil for frying

Preparation: Place all ingredients into a bowl and knead them by hand until you have a smooth dough. Form pancakes out of small portions of dough, place them on a baking tray greased with oil and bake them in the oven at 200 degrees Celsius for 20 minutes. Flip the pancakes once while they are baking in the oven. Alternatively, fry the pancakes in some oil on both sides in a pan until golden yellow. Serve the pancakes together with e.g. fresh salads, steamed spinach, steamed chard or steamed curly kale (also known as "green cabbage"). Cold potato pancakes can also be served as a snack or at a buffet—together with a homemade lentil, bean or chickpea spread, topped with sliced peppers, fresh tomatoes, cucumbers or chayotes or sprinkled with chives.

Potato pancakes, prepared with raw potatoes:

Ingredients: 4 organic waxy potatoes, ½ cup of steamed organic millet or buckwheat, 3–4 tablespoons of organic wholemeal buckwheat flour, ½ teaspoon of organic spices such as marjoram, wild garlic, caraway and some ground or grated nutmeg, fresh herbs together with onion and garlic leaves in summer, ¼ tablespoon of natural rock salt, heat-resistant organic olive or sunflower oil for frying

Preparation: Peel and grate the raw potatoes and knead them by hand together with all other ingredients in a bowl until a dough forms. The rest of the procedure is the same as for the potato pancakes prepared with boiled potatoes.

Potato-buckwheat or potato-millet pizza:

Ingredients: ½ kg of organic waxy potatoes that have been boiled, peeled and pressed through a potato ricer, ½ cup of boiled organic millet or buckwheat, 5 tablespoons of organic buckwheat flour, some water, ¼ teaspoon of each of the following organic spices: caraway, wild garlic spice and marjoram, some ground or grated organic nutmeg, ¼ tablespoon of natural rock salt; ingredients used to sprinkle on the dough: dried organic spices or fresh, finely chopped organic herbs (paprika powder, caraway, rosemary, oregano, the leaves of hardy onions and garlic, wild garlic and/or sunflower seeds, chopped pumpkin seeds without traces of gluten); heat-resistant organic oil for the baking tray or environmentally friendly baking parchment

Preparation: Knead all ingredients by hand until a dough forms. Place the dough on a baking tray greased with oil and press from the centre outwards with your wet hands until the dough is 1 cm thick. Sprinkle the surface alternately with spices, herbs and seeds and press them lightly into the dough. Bake the pizza in the preheated oven at 180 degrees Celsius for 40 minutes.

Afterwards, take the baking tray out of the oven, place it outside and allow it to stand briefly. Finally, cut the pizza into small pieces.

Potato-buckwheat or potato-millet pizza with toppings:

Ingredients: Prepare a potato dough with the ingredients described above. For a herbal topping: ½ kg of organic spinach, chard or wild garlic, ½ teaspoon of organic marjoram, some ground or grated organic nutmeg, some natural rock salt; for a vegetable topping: 4 organic tomatoes, 1 organic courgette, organic spices such as oregano, basil, wild garlic and savoury, the leaves of hardy onions and garlic, some natural rock salt; heat-resistant organic oil for the baking tray.

Preparation: Press the potato dough onto a baking tray as described above and spread briefly steamed spinach, chard or wild garlic across the dough.

In case of a vegetable topping: Spread the raw and finely chopped vegetables across the dough, salt them a little and sprinkle spices over the top. The rest of the procedure is the same as for the previous recipe.

In natural storage conditions, the potato season ends as soon as the potatoes start to sprout and only begins again when there are seasonal and regional "new potatoes" with many minerals, such as silicon, etc. The nitrogen-stored and mostly irradiated potatoes of the previous year are energetically dead.

Salads

Chayote salad:

Ingredients: 1 chayote, 2 organic apples, some organic pumpkin seed oil or virgin organic fruity olive oil (very healthy due to omega-3 fatty acids), ½ organic lemon or organic sea buckthorn juice, some natural rock salt, some coarsely chopped and roasted organic walnuts

Preparation: Gently peel the chayote. Cut the unpeeled apples and the peeled chayote into small sticks and dress the salad in a bowl with organic oil, organic lemon or sea buckthorn juice and some salt. Before serving the salad, pour a little pumpkin seed oil in a nice pattern over it and sprinkle chopped walnuts over it. Chayotes can be mixed into all salads. They are especially tasty in a potato salad. Chayotes provide valuable minerals and many vitamins, which is particularly beneficial in winter. Please do not eat sprouting chayotes any more, but plant them in your own garden in spring or give them away to someone else for their garden.

Jerusalem artichoke salad:

Ingredients: 4 Jerusalem artichoke tubers, ½ organic lemon, some natural rock salt, organic pumpkin seed oil or virgin organic fruity olive oil
Preparation: Clean the Jerusalem artichoke tubers with a vegetable brush under running water and grate them finely. Dress the finely grated tubers with freshly squeezed lemon juice, some salt and oil. This raw food is also a very special source of minerals. Grated Jerusalem artichokes can be mixed into all salads, just like chayotes.

Dandelion salad with organic beans or organic lentils:

Ingredients: freshly harvested dandelion leaves and buds, 1 cup of boiled organic beans or organic lentils, ½ cup of steamed millet or some boiled organic waxy potatoes, chives or onion and garlic leaves, organic pumpkin seed oil or organic fruity olive oil, 1 organic lemon or organic sea buckthorn juice, some natural rock salt.
Preparation: Place the washed and finely chopped dandelion greens, the boiled beans/lentils, the steamed millet or the peeled and thinly sliced potatoes into a bowl. Dress the salad with oil, the juice of an organic lemon or sea buckthorn juice, natural rock salt and optionally some herbal tea or soup.

Leaf lettuces or leaf lettuces with leafy vegetables:

Ingredients: 1 large bowl of leaf lettuces or 1 small bowl of leaf lettuces and 1 bowl of leafy vegetables such as mallow leaves, watercress leaves and flowers, New Zealand spinach leaves and tender dandelion leaves, either 1 cup of steamed organic millet, 4 soft-boiled and peeled organic potatoes or 1 cup of soft-steamed organic beans or lentils, 1 organic lemon or organic sea buckthorn juice, organic pumpkin seed oil or organic fruity olive oil, some natural rock salt and optionally some herbal tea or soup
Preparation: Wash the leaf lettuces or the leaf lettuces and the leafy vegetables, cut them into small strips and place them into a salad bowl together with either 1 cup of steamed millet or 4 soft-boiled, peeled and thinly

sliced potatoes or 1 cup of soft-steamed beans or lentils. Dress the salad with the juice of an organic lemon or sea buckthorn juice, salt, organic oil and optionally some soup or herbal tea.

Rocket salad:

Ingredients: 1 bowl of rocket; the other ingredients can be the same as in the leaf lettuces.

Preparation: Prepared in the same way as the leaf lettuces. As an alternative, mix seasonal tomatoes cut into small pieces into the salad and sprinkle roasted walnuts over it.

Salad made of edible wild herbs and flowers:

Ingredients: Edible wild herbs and flowers, 5 boiled organic waxy potatoes or ½ cup of steamed organic millet, leftovers of boiled legumes (if available), some soup or herbal tea, 1 tablespoon of wild garlic spice or fresh chives, fresh onion and garlic leaves, some natural rock salt, organic pumpkin seed oil or organic fruity olive oil, 1 organic lemon or organic sea buckthorn juice

Preparation: Wash and finely chop the edible wild herbs and flowers you have collected. (If you are unsure which plants are edible, get a plant guide.) Place them into a bowl together with the warm, peeled and sliced potatoes or ½ cup of steamed millet and optionally with the leftovers of boiled legumes. Dress the salad with fresh garden herbs, salt, optionally some soup or herbal tea and the juice of an organic lemon or sea buckthorn juice. Sprinkle fresh colourful flowers over the salad and enjoy.

Potato salad:

Ingredients: ½ kg of organic waxy potatoes, some caraway, the leaves of hardy onions and garlic, organic pumpkin seed oil or organic fruity olive oil, 1 organic lemon or organic sea buckthorn juice, leftovers of soup or some herbal tea, ½ teaspoon of natural rock salt

Preparation: Put the potatoes into a pot, cover them with water and bring them to the boil. Now, turn down to the second lowest heat and boil the potatoes for about 25 minutes until soft. Afterwards, peel the potatoes, allow them to cool and cut them into thin slices. Place the thinly sliced potatoes into a salad bowl and dress them with oil, the juice of an organic lemon or sea

buckthorn juice, caraway, onion and garlic leaves and some cold soup or cold herbal tea. If you have a homemade lentil, chickpea or bean spread to hand, alternatively stir 1 tablespoon of spread into the salad.
You can prepare a colourful potato salad using the additional ingredients of ½ chayote, cut into small sticks, 1 finely grated Jerusalem artichoke tuber, 1 apple, cut into small sticks, diced tomatoes and 1 handful of chopped rocket.

Desserts (from the 5th week onward only)

Apples or pears baked on a baking tray:

Ingredients: organic apples or organic pears, some water
Preparation: Wash the apples or pears and place them on a baking tray with some water. Put the baking tray into the oven preheated to 200 degrees Celsius and bake the apples or pears in the oven for about 30 minutes. As soon as their skins start to burst, take them out of the oven and allow them to cool. Enjoy for breakfast, as a dessert or for dinner together with some steamed millet.

Apple or pear sauce:

Ingredients: organic apples or organic pears (or both), some water
Preparation: Wash the apples and/or pears, core them, but leave the peel on them and cut them into pieces. Put the fruit and some water into a pot and bring the water to the boil. Turn down to the lowest heat and steam the fruit for about 3–4 minutes. Afterwards, beat the fruit with a whisk until creamy and fill it into screw cap jars while it is still hot. This preserved sauce stays good for a very long time and does not need to be kept in the refrigerator.

Stewed seasonal fruits (compote):

Ingredients: seasonal organic fruits, water
Preparation: Wash the seasonal organic fruits, core them and, if appropriate, cut them into pieces. Put the fruits into a cooking pot, cover them with water and bring the water to the boil. Turn down to the lowest heat and stew the fruits for about 2 minutes. Fill the compote into screw cap jars while it is still hot. These preserved stewed fruits stay good for a very long time and can be stored as a supply for the winter.

Juicy berry sauce: (may also serve as a supply for the winter)

Ingredients: seasonal berries (strawberries, raspberries, bilberries, blueberries, blackberries)

Preparation: Wash the berries well and stew them a little in a covered pot. Afterwards, either press the berries through a sieve or drive them through a straining machine to remove the seeds. Bring the berry sauce to the boil and fill it into clean screw cap jars while it is still hot. Hot-filled berry sauce stays good for a very long time without adding sugar or preservatives.

Fruit sauce and fruity treats for children made of seasonal fruit:

Ingredients: homemade gelling aid made of quinces or 1 teaspoon of agar-agar (2 teaspoons of agar-agar for the sweet treats), 1 kg of seasonal fruit

Preparation of the gelling aid: Core quinces harvested in autumn, but leave the peel on them, cut them into small pieces and stew them with a tiny bit of water until soft. Drive the stewed quince pieces through a mechanical straining machine and bring the strained quinces to the boil once more. Afterwards, fill the gelling aid into screw cap jars while it is still hot.

Preparation of the fruit sauce: Wash the berries (strawberries, raspberries, bilberries, blueberries, etc.). Core the seasonal fruit (apples, pears, apricots, plums, etc.) and cut it into small pieces. Stir a tiny bit of water and the gelling aid made of quinces (the quantity you use depends on the consistency you want to achieve) or 1 teaspoon of agar-agar into the fruit. Bring the mixture to the boil in a covered cooking pot. Remove the lid and let the mixture simmer over the lowest heat for 2 minutes (stir once in a while). Afterwards, mash the fruit with a potato masher and fill the sauce into screw cap jars while it is still hot. In winter and spring, when there is no seasonal, fresh fruit, this sauce can be enjoyed as a dessert. It also tastes great as a filling in pancakes.

Preparation of the fruity treats for children: Prepare the sweet treats in the same way as the fruit sauce, but add a little more gelling aid made of quinces or agar-agar to the fruit. (Be careful with the dosage of agar-agar, it has a very strong gelling power.) Pour the boiled, hot fruit mass into a flat glass casserole dish or into various biscuit cutters on a baking tray. Allow the fruit mass to cool down completely in a cold place (until it has solidified). Afterwards, cut the fruit mass into small pieces or press the fruity treats out of the biscuit cutters. In summer you can stick wooden handles into the biscuit figures, place them into a bowl and put them briefly into the freezer. This would be a healthy alternative to ice cream with lots of sugar, additives and flavour enhancers. At children's birthday parties, such creatively prepared treats are always very popular—not only with parents (who are pleased when their children are offered healthy food), but also with children.

Apple, pear or bilberry/blueberry bake:

Ingredients: 1 cup of steamed organic millet, 1 cup of ground or grated organic nuts, ¼ teaspoon of natural rock salt; topping: ½ kg of organic apples, ½ kg of organic pears, ½ kg of organic bilberries/blueberries or forest bilberries/blueberries (seasonal organic fruits), optionally 5 dried apricots in case of an apple or pear bake, heat-resistant organic oil for the baking tray
Preparation: Place the steamed millet, the nuts and the salt into a bowl and stir them with a wooden spoon. Place the dough into an oven-proof dish greased with oil and press from the centre outwards with your wet hands until the dough is 1 cm thick. Squeeze the juice out of the grated apples or pears and spread the apples/pears (optionally mix chopped, washed dried apricots into the apples or pears) or the bilberries/blueberries (the seasonal fruit) across the dough. Bake the fruit bake in the preheated oven at 200 degrees Celsius (top and bottom heat) for about 35 minutes (until the outer edges are crunchy). Afterwards, take the bake out of the oven, place it outside and allow it to stand briefly.

Energy balls: (provide magnesium, selenium, zinc, iron ...)

Energy balls can also be used in case of chocolate addiction and cravings for sweets.
Ingredients: 200 g of dried organic apricots (or organic plums), 1 cup of roasted and ground or grated organic walnuts, 2 tablespoons of organic coconut oil, the juice of half of a lemon, 1 tablespoon of organic cocoa, organic coconut flakes or grated walnuts
Preparation: Wash the dried apricots well under the sink, put them into a cooking pot and cover them with water. Bring the water to the boil and stew the apricots over the lowest heat for about 10 minutes until soft. Mash the stewed apricots with a potato masher und blend the mush until smooth using a wooden spoon or drive the stewed apricots through a mechanical straining

machine. Allow the apricot sauce to cool a little, then stir in the other ingredients (except the organic coconut flakes or grated walnuts) and put this dough in a cold place. Pour the organic coconut flakes or grated walnuts into a bowl, form small balls from the dough and roll the balls in the coconut flakes or grated walnuts. Store these life and root force-strengthening goodies in a cold place and enjoy them when you need an energy boost.

Oven-baked goodies (from the 5th week onward, except the oleaginous fruit bread, which can be eaten from the 2nd week onward)

All ingredients in the recipes are powerful sources of energy and minerals for a healthy growth, especially for children, people suffering from stress and athletes who have increased mineral and energy requirements. The spices used stimulate digestion and self-healing. Psyllium husk flakes swell up to 20 times their volume and heal the stomach and intestines.
If you have a grain mill with a natural stone at home, you should always freshly grind buckwheat, millet, Seewinkler natural rice (from Seewinkel in Austria) or large brown lentils when you need flour. If you are allergic to buckwheat, you can use millet flour, brown lentil flour or Seewinkler natural rice flour in recipes using buckwheat flour. You can also flour the baking tray or tin with millet or rice flour; alternatively, you can use environmentally friendly baking parchment.

<u>Oleaginous fruit bread:</u> (provides an enormous amount of energy, satiates and is ideal for those who want to burn fat)
Ingredients: 1 cup of buckwheat flour (contains a lot of oil), 1 cup of grated nuts or pumpkin seeds, ½ cup of each of the following seeds: coarsely ground linseed, whole sesame seeds and sunflower seeds (make sure that these seeds do not contain traces of gluten), 4 tablespoons of psyllium husk flakes, ½ tablespoon of natural rock salt, 1 teaspoon of each of the following seeds: caraway, fennel and ground or grated coriander, mineral water with natural carbonic acid and a high iodine content, environmentally friendly baking parchment for the baking tray

Preparation: Mix all dry ingredients well in a large bowl and stir, pouring in water until a juicy lump of dough forms. Place the dough on a parchment-lined baking tray with your wet hands, form a loaf with your wet hands and sprinkle it with sesame seeds (press the seeds lightly into the dough). Before or while preparing the dough, preheat the oven to 200 degrees Celsius. Place the baking tray on the middle shelf of the oven and turn down the heat to 190 degrees Celsius. Bake the bread for about 50 to 60 minutes. Afterwards, place it on a wire rack covered with a tea towel and leave it to cool.

<u>Spice bread:</u>

Ingredients: 1 cup of organic wholemeal buckwheat flour, 5 tablespoons of organic wholemeal millet flour without traces of gluten, 2 cups of ground or grated organic nuts (or 1 cup of ground or grated organic walnuts and 1 cup of ground or grated organic pumpkin seeds), 3 tablespoons of organic psyllium husks, ½ tablespoon of natural rock salt, ½ teaspoon of each of the following organic seeds: caraway, fennel and ground or grated coriander (at your discretion, you may add 1 tablespoon of organic oregano or organic wild garlic spice as well as roasted organic onion and/or garlic leaves in summer), 1 tablespoon of heat-resistant organic oil, mineral water high in sodium, environmentally friendly baking parchment for a baking tray or heat-resistant organic oil and some organic buckwheat flour for a baking tin—try to mix pumpkin seeds, sunflower seeds or linseed without traces of gluten into the dough

Preparation: Place all dry ingredients into a bowl and mix them well. Afterwards, add the oil and stir with a wooden spoon, pouring in water until a lump of dough forms.

Grease an oven-proof dish with oil and flour it with buckwheat flour. Place the dough into an oven-proof dish. Alternatively, form a loaf, place it on a parchment-lined baking tray, smoothen it with your wet hands and optionally sprinkle it with linseed. Before or while preparing the dough, preheat the oven to 200 degrees Celsius. Place a wire rack on the lowest shelf of the oven and put the oven-proof dish on the rack or place the baking tray on the middle shelf of the oven, turn down the heat to 190 degrees Celsius and bake the bread for about 50 to 60 minutes. Cover a wire rack with a tea towel, take the bread out of the oven and turn it out onto the rack. Wrap the bread in the tea towel and leave it to cool. This bread is a culinary delight.

Succulent apple bread:

Ingredients: ½ cup of organic wholemeal buckwheat flour, ½ cup of organic brown lentil flour, 2 tablespoons of organic browntop millet without traces of gluten, 3 tablespoons of psyllium husk flakes, ½ tablespoon of natural rock salt, ½ teaspoon of each of the following organic seeds: caraway, fennel and ground or grated coriander, 1 apple, 2 tablespoons of heat-resistant organic oil, mineral water high in sodium, heat-resistant organic oil and wholemeal buckwheat flour for a baking tin or environmentally friendly baking parchment for a baking tray

Preparation: Mix all dry ingredients well in a bowl. Add the apple coarsely grated with a slicer and 2 tablespoons of oil and pour in water until you can stir the dough with a wooden spoon. Place the dough into a baking tin greased with oil and floured with buckwheat flour. Alternatively, form a loaf and place it on a parchment-lined baking tray. Before or while preparing the dough, preheat the oven to 200 degrees Celsius. Place a wire rack on the lowest shelf of the oven and put the baking tin on the rack or place the baking tray on the middle shelf of the oven. Turn down the heat to 190 degrees Celsius and bake the bread for about 50 to 60 minutes. Proceed as usual for allowing the bread to cool. Because of the lentil flour, this bread provides a lot of protein.

Crusty bread baked on a baking tray:

Ingredients: 1 cup of organic wholemeal buckwheat flour, 2 tablespoons of organic browntop millet without traces of gluten, 1 cup of ground or grated organic nuts (or ½ cup of ground or grated organic walnuts and ½ cup of ground or grated organic pumpkin seeds), 2 tablespoons of heat-resistant organic oil, 1 teaspoon of natural rock salt, ¼ teaspoon of each of the following organic spices: caraway, fennel, savoury or oregano and ground or grated coriander seeds, 4 tablespoons of coarsely ground organic linseed, 4 tablespoons of organic sunflower seeds without traces of gluten or 4 tablespoons of chopped organic walnuts, mineral water with natural carbonic acid and a high sodium content; ingredients used to sprinkle on the

dough: organic caraway seeds, organic wild garlic spice or coarsely ground organic linseed; environmentally friendly baking parchment for the baking tray
Preparation: Place all dry ingredients into a bowl and mix them well. Afterwards, add the oil and pour in water until you can stir a smooth dough with a wooden spoon. Place the dough on a parchment-lined baking tray. Smooth the dough down from the centre outwards with your wet hands until the dough is ½ cm thick. Dip your hands in water and moisten the dough with water. Afterwards, sprinkle the dough with caraway seeds and wild garlic spice and/or coarsely ground linseed. Bake the dough in the preheated oven at 200 degrees Celsius for about 30 minutes (until it has taken on some colour at the bottom). Afterwards, take the crusty bread out of the oven and allow it to stand in the open air. Finally, cut the bread into small pieces.

Courgette, fresh fruit or dried fruit bread:

Ingredients: 1 cup of organic wholemeal buckwheat flour, ½ cup of organic wholemeal millet flour without traces of gluten, 2 cups of ground or grated organic nuts, 3 tablespoons of organic psyllium husks, ½ tablespoon of natural rock salt, ½ teaspoon of organic caraway, ½ teaspoon of organic fennel, ¼ teaspoon of organic clove powder and ground or grated organic coriander seeds, some grated peel of an organic lemon, 1 coarsely grated small organic courgette, 2 tablespoons of heat-resistant organic oil, mineral water with natural carbonic acid and a high sodium content, environmentally friendly baking parchment for the baking tray (if applicable)
For a fresh fruit bread, use 1 grated pear or apple, 5 chopped apricots and chopped cherries, chopped plums or ½ cup of bilberries/blueberries. For a dried fruit bread, use ½ kg of chopped dried pears and ¼ kg of chopped dried apricots and/or plums.
Preparation: Place all dry ingredients into a bowl and mix them well. Afterwards, add either the courgette or the fresh fruit or the dried fruit as well as the oil and pour in water until you can form a lump of dough with your hands. Place the dough into an oven-proof dish greased with oil and floured with buckwheat flour. Alternatively, form a loaf and place it on a parchment-lined baking tray. Before or while preparing the dough, preheat the oven to 200 degrees Celsius. Place a wire rack on the lowest shelf of the oven and put the oven-proof dish on the rack or place the baking tray on the middle shelf of

the oven, turn down the heat to 190 degrees Celsius and bake the bread for about 50 to 60 minutes. (The longer the baking time, the thicker the crust.) Cover a wire rack with a tea towel, take the bread out of the oven and turn it out onto the rack. Wrap the bread in the tea towel and leave it to cool. The swelling of the psyllium husks makes this bread succulent and fluffy.

Sweet or savoury snacks made with buckwheat and millet flour:

Ingredients for the dough: 1 cup or organic wholemeal buckwheat flour, ½ cup of organic millet flour, ½ cup of organic wholemeal millet flour (unhusked golden millet) without traces of gluten, 2 cups of ground or grated organic nuts, 1 tablespoon of organic psyllium husks, 5 tablespoons of heat-resistant organic sunflower oil, some natural rock salt, water, 1 pinch of clove powder (for sweet biscuits or a cake only), 2 tablespoons of ground or grated organic walnuts (for sweet biscuits only), optionally 1 cup of organic apple or pear sauce (for sweet biscuits or a cake only)

Additional ingredients (organic spices and seeds) for savoury biscuits: E.g. wild garlic, basil, oregano, savoury, caraway, fennel, linseed, sunflower seeds and/or pumpkin seeds

Additional ingredients for cake variations: 1 kg of coarsely grated organic apples; 1 kg of sliced organic pears or apricots; 1 kg of organic bilberries/blueberries; 1 kg of halved cherries; 1 kg of halved or quartered plums; heat-resistant organic oil for the baking tray (if applicable)

Preparation: Place all dry ingredients for the dough into a bowl and mix them well with a wooden spoon. Afterwards add the oil and optionally add the fruit sauce. Stir with the wooden spoon, pouring in water until a thick lump of dough forms.

For sweet biscuits, liberally sprinkle buckwheat flour on a kitchen worktop. Roll the dough in the buckwheat flour and roll it out with a wooden rolling pin until it is 5 mm thick. Brush the rolled dough with some water, sprinkle it with grated walnuts and cut out round biscuits with a wine glass.

For savoury biscuits, knead all spices and finely chopped seeds into the dough. Liberally sprinkle buckwheat flour on a kitchen worktop, roll the dough in the flour and roll it out as described above. Brush the rolled dough with some water, sprinkle it with caraway seeds, fennel seeds and linseed and cut out round biscuits.

Place the sweet or savoury biscuits on a baking tray greased with oil and floured with buckwheat flour or lined with environmentally friendly baking parchment. Bake the biscuits in the preheated oven at 200 degrees Celsius for about 10 minutes (until they have taken on some colour at the bottom).
For a cake, place half of the dough (prepared according to the basic recipe) on a baking tray greased with oil and floured with buckwheat flour or lined with environmentally friendly baking parchment. Flatten the dough from the centre outwards with your wet hands until the dough is 5 mm thick. Spread grated apples, sliced pears, sliced apricots, bilberries/blueberries, halved cherries or halved or quartered plums across the flattened dough. Roll out the second half of the dough to 5 mm thick, quarter it with a knife, place the rolled dough quarters over the fruit and press them down lightly. Bake the cake in the preheated oven at 200 degrees Celsius for 40 to 45 minutes.

Gingerbread:
Ingredients: 1 cup of organic wholemeal buckwheat flour, ½ cup of organic millet flour, 2 tablespoons of organic wholemeal millet flour without traces of gluten, 2 cups of ground or grated organic nuts, 1 tablespoon of organic psyllium husk flakes, 5 tablespoons of heat-resistant organic sunflower or rapeseed oil, some natural rock salt, ¼ teaspoon of clove powder, cardamom, aniseed, ground or grated coriander seeds, ground or grated nutmeg, optionally 250 g of dried apricots for a sweet flavour, sodium-rich mineral water; ingredients used to sprinkle or spread on the dough: grated or halved walnuts; heat-resistant organic oil or environmentally friendly baking parchment for the baking tray
Preparation: Stew the dried apricots with a little water until they are very soft. Afterwards, mash them with a potato masher and stir them with a wooden spoon until a spreadable paste forms. Allow the paste to cool. Place all dry ingredients for the dough into a bowl and mix them well with a wooden spoon. Afterwards, add the oil and the cooled apricot paste. Pour in sodium-rich mineral water until you can form a dough with your hands. Prepare the dough quickly; it should not be too soft. Liberally sprinkle buckwheat flour on a kitchen worktop. Roll the dough in the buckwheat flour and roll it out with a wooden rolling pin until it is 5 mm thick. Brush the rolled dough with some water, sprinkle it with grated walnuts and cut out hearts, stars, etc. with biscuit

cutters. (Alternatively, cut out the biscuits after rolling out the dough, place a walnut half on top of each biscuit and press the walnut halves lightly into the dough.) Place the biscuits on a baking tray greased with oil and floured with buckwheat flour or lined with environmentally friendly baking parchment. Bake the biscuits in the preheated oven at 200 degrees Celsius for about 10 minutes (until they have taken on some colour at the bottom).

Fruit cake (baked on a baking tray or in a cake tin):

Ingredients: 1 cup or organic wholemeal buckwheat flour, 5 tablespoons of organic browntop millet flour without traces of gluten, 2 cups of ground or grated organic nuts, ¼ teaspoon of natural rock salt, ¼ teaspoon of clove powder, 2 tablespoons of organic psyllium husks, 3 tablespoons of heat-resistant organic oil, sodium-rich mineral water, 1 ½ kg of seasonal organic fruits (apples, pears, apricots, bilberries/blueberries, cherries, plums, etc.), 1 tablespoon of agar-agar; heat-resistant organic oil or environmentally friendly baking parchment for the baking tray

Preparation: Mix all dry ingredients well in a bowl. Afterwards, add the oil and pour in water until you can stir a smooth dough with a wooden spoon. Place the dough either into a cake tin greased with oil and floured with buckwheat flour or on a parchment-lined baking tray. Smoothen the dough with your wet hands. Before or while preparing the dough, preheat the oven to 200 degrees Celsius. Bake the cake for 35 minutes in the cake tin or for about 30 minutes on the baking tray. While the cake is baking in the oven, wash the fruits, core them if necessary and cut them into small pieces. Moisten a pot with some water, put the fruits into the pot, stir in the agar-agar and stew the fruits in the covered pot until soft. You can also drive fruits like apples and pears through a mechanical straining machine. Once the cake has slightly cooled down in the cake tin or on the baking tray, spread the fruits or the fruit sauce over the cake and smoothen them/it with a knife. Once the fruit mass has solidified, take the cake out of the tin or cube it on the baking tray. Afterwards, offer the fruit cake on a serving plate.

Oven-baked creations (not only) for people allergic to buckwheat

Bread made with millet and lentil flour:

Ingredients: 1 cup of organic millet flour, 2 tablespoons of organic wholemeal millet flour (browntop millet), 1 cup of freshly ground organic large brown lentils without traces of gluten (use your grain mill for grinding gluten-free cereals and lentils only), 1 cup of freshly ground or grated organic walnuts, 4 tablespoons of organic psyllium husk flakes, ½ teaspoon of each of the following organic seeds: caraway, fennel and ground or grated coriander, 1 teaspoon of natural rock salt, 2 tablespoons of heat-resistant organic oil, mineral water with natural carbonic acid and a high sodium content, heat-resistant organic oil and organic buckwheat flour for a baking tin or environmentally friendly baking parchment for a baking tray
Preparation: Mix all dry ingredients well in a large bowl. Afterwards, add the oil and pour in water until you can stir a dough with a wooden spoon. Before or while preparing the dough, preheat the oven to 200 degrees Celsius. Place the dough into a baking tin greased with oil and floured with millet flour. Alternatively, form a loaf and place it on a parchment-lined baking tray. Place a wire rack on the lowest shelf of the oven and put the baking tin on the rack. Alternatively, place the baking tray on the middle shelf of the oven. Turn down the heat to 190 degrees Celsius and bake the bread for about 50 to 60 minutes. Proceed as usual for allowing the bread to cool.

Millet & fruit cake:

Ingredients: 1 cup of freshly ground or grated organic walnuts or peeled organic almonds, 1 cup of organic millet flour, ¼ teaspoon of natural rock salt, 3 tablespoons of organic psyllium husk flakes, 2 tablespoons of heat-resistant organic oil, natural mineral water high in sodium, heat-resistant organic oil and organic millet flour for the cake tin; 250 g of dried organic apricots, 2 tablespoons of organic coconut oil, seasonal organic fruits (in winter e.g. 4 organic kiwis), ½ l of apple sauce, 1 flat tablespoon of agar-agar, some water
Preparation: Mix all dry ingredients well in a bowl. Afterwards, add the oil and pour in water until you can stir a juicy dough with a wooden spoon. Place this dough into a springform pan greased with oil and floured with millet flour. Before or while preparing the dough, preheat the oven to 200 degrees Celsius.

Place a wire rack on the lowest shelf of the oven and put the springform pan on the rack. Bake the cake base at 190 degrees Celsius for about 40 minutes. Open the springform pan, turn the cake out onto a cake serving plate and leave it to cool.
Put the dried apricots into a cooking pot and cover them with water. Bring the water to the boil and stew the apricots for 5 minutes. Afterwards, mash the apricots with a potato masher or drive them through a straining machine and blend the mush until smooth using a wooden spoon. Allow the apricot mush to cool. Stir 2 tablespoons of coconut oil into the cooled apricot mush. Cut the cake in the middle and fill it with the cooled apricot mush. Peel the kiwis and cut them into round pieces. Spread the kiwis (or the seasonal fruits) over the cake. Place the ring of the springform pan around the cake. Pour the apple sauce into a cooking pot, stir in agar-agar and heat the apple sauce to the boiling point. Afterwards, pour the apple sauce over the kiwis (or the seasonal fruits) and smoothen it with a knife. Once the cake has slightly cooled down, cut out a figure (e.g. a heart) in the middle of a sheet of baking parchment, place the sheet on the cake and sprinkle coconut flakes into the cut figure. Afterwards, carefully lift the sheet. Once the apple sauce has solidified, remove the ring of the springform pan. This fruity and succulent cake is a hit at every birthday party.

5.8. Babies fed organic, root and life force-strengthening food experience comprehensively healthy growth

Up to six months of age, babies only need breast milk. The composition of breast milk constantly adapts to the changing needs of the growing child.
From six to twelve months of age, breast milk can be reduced and the baby can gradually be offered more and more root and life force-strengthening mushy organic food. During this time, many mothers only breastfeed their baby in the morning and evening. From 12 months of age onwards, breast milk provides almost no nutrients to the child. As nature intended, the baby, which then usually already has teeth, separates from the breast as a source of food.

If a baby cannot be breastfed, you can prepare a breast milk-like life and root force-strengthening organic formula for bottle feeding on your own. The recipe originates from macrobiotics. (Please note: This formula is *not* intended to *replace* breast milk. If you are unable to breastfeed your child, please talk to your paediatrician or midwife about breast milk substitutes.)

Ingredients for the macrobiotic, organic formula for bottle feeding: 1 cup of Seewinkler natural organic rice (from Seewinkel in Austria), ½ cup of organic golden millet, ¼ cup of organic lentils or organic beans, ¼ cup of organic sunflower seeds without traces of gluten, ¼ cup of organic sesame seeds without traces of gluten, 10 cups of water
Preparation: Leave the beans to soak overnight. Lentils do not need to be soaked overnight. The next day, strain the soaking water from the beans and use it to water the flowers. Rinse the lentils or beans, the millet and the rice vigorously with hot water under the sink. Pour all ingredients, including the water, into a pot, bring them to the boil and let them simmer over the lowest heat for 3 hours in the covered pot. Stir the mush from time to time during cooking. Afterwards, press the mush through a sieve with a very fine mesh and then through a diaper. Dispose of the fibre with the organic waste. (The essence is contained in the liquid.) If the liquid is still too thick for bottle feeding, add more water (according to the desired consistency) and bring the baby food to the boil again, stirring from time to time. Afterwards, strain the baby food once more and fill it portion by portion into clean screw cap jars with non-toxic, PVC-free caps (recognisable by a blue ring in the cap) while it is still hot. Allow the baby food to cool and store it in the refrigerator for no more than a week. Always warm the food before giving it to the baby.

Babies who cannot be breastfed pass a normal, healthy poop with this root and life force-strengthening organic formula for bottle feeding; their metabolism works like a charm and their poop smells similar to breast milk. Babies fed in this way are very lively and soon begin to raise their head. They sleep well and cry loudly when they are hungry (my own experience with a grandchild).
If you prepare this basic organic formula with less water, it is also ideal for supplementary feeding from six months of age onwards and for switching from breast and bottle feeding to spoon feeding (porridge with fruits or vegetables).

In this case, instead of 10 cups, take only 5 cups of water. After cooking, drive the mush through a straining machine with a fine mesh and dispose of the fibre with the organic waste. Bring the food to the boil again and fill it into screw cap jars with PVC-free caps while it is still hot. Allow the food to cool and store it in the refrigerator for no more than one week.
For a porridge meal, mix fruit or vegetable sauce and ½ teaspoon of cold-pressed organic oil with omega-3 fatty acids particularly designed for babies (80% should be organic rapeseed oil) with the basic formula and feed it to the baby with an untreated (wooden) spoon while it is still warm.
Babies love this organic baby food if they have not been fed any ready-made products from the beginning. My older daughter prepared this baby food for her son from six months of age onwards, after she had to wean him. Her son accepted the food immediately and he developed very well with it.
For midday meals, mix steamed organic squash or pumpkin (which you purée at the beginning—babies especially love sweet red kuri squash), chayote, potatoes or steamed and puréed spring herbs from the meadow or garden herbs with the basic formula; for breakfast or dinner, mix stewed local, seasonal and organic fruits and ½ teaspoon of cold-pressed organic oil with omega-3 fatty acids particularly designed for babies with the basic formula. In this way, babies become adapted to more solid food and soon start to eat porridge made from organic golden millet or from organic buckwheat (whole grains) as well as organic buckwheat *Sterz* (traditional rural dish made from cereals) from the family pot of food. My grandchildren ate everything from the life and root force-strengthening family pot of food when they were only one year old.
Important note: Decisions on how to feed a child are the personal responsibility of their parents.

5.9. Things to consider after dental surgery if you have chewing or swallowing problems

- Avoid down pillows and duvets (only use pillows and blankets made of organic cotton and filled with organic virgin wool pearls)
- Protect yourself from draughts and wind (also from air conditioning in cars)
- Do not consume milk and milk products or animal protein

- Perform mouthwashes with cooled but not extremely cold tea for wound healing
- If you have chewing problems, consume mushy organic food with strong life and root forces

Tea recipes for wound-healing mouthwashes

Ingredients: water, organic chamomile blossoms, organic marsh-mallow leaves, organic pot marigolds or organic sage

Preparation: Heat the water in a cooking pot to the boiling point. Put 1 tablespoon of chamomile blossoms and 1 tablespoon of marsh-mallow leaves, pot marigolds or sage into a teapot made of glass or ceramic and pour the hot water over the blossoms and herbs. Let the tea brew for 10 minutes. Afterwards, strain the tea with a tea sieve and put it in a cold place. Use only cold tea for mouthwashes.

Life and root force-strengthening drink

Ingredients: 1 cup of organic beans (I recommend organic soya beans to women with menopausal symptoms if it is possible to obtain soybeans grown in pure stands) or 1 cup of organic lentils, ½ cup of organic sunflower seeds without traces of gluten, ½ cup of organic sesame seeds without traces of gluten, organic meadow herbs such as stinging nettle tips, ground ivy and dandelion, seasonal organic garden herbs such as chard, curly kale (also known as "green cabbage") leaves, parsley, carrot leaves, oregano and marjoram, 3 litres of water

Preparation: Pour all ingredients except the meadow and garden herbs into a pot, bring them to the boil and let them simmer over the lowest heat for 3 hours. Afterwards, add the meadow and garden herbs, bring the drink to the boiling point again, let it simmer lightly for 10 minutes, strain it with a sieve and fill it into ¼ l screw cap jars while it is still hot. Drink it every day for one week—three times the first day and then once a day. Purée the strained ingredients and add them to soups, sauces or patties. (This drink is also suitable for regeneration in case of serious diseases and for old people.)

If you suffer from chewing and swallowing problems, it is particularly important to eat organic food that strengthens life and root forces and unlocks your self-healing powers. You can find many recipes that are also suitable for chewing and swallowing problems in the nutrition section of this book.

5.10. Healthy lifestyle and eating habits can contribute substantially to well-being

While preparing food and eating, you should be **careful**, **sensual** and **stress-free**. This is very important.

Stomach and bowel care starts at your nose; appetite for food is stimulated by its pleasant odour. Never eat without being hungry because “hunger is the best relish”.

“After dinner rest a while, after supper walk a mile.”

A German proverb says, “The bowel goes to sleep with the chickens and gets up with the chickens”. This means that the physical biorhythm causes the digestive system to rest during the night. For this reason, you should not eat anything late in the evening and, most importantly, you should not eat anything raw before going to bed.

A healthy digestion starts with a healthy (i.e. fully restored, where applicable) set of teeth. Take small bites out of your food and chew them properly until they feel like a purée in your mouth. Do not drink during meals, i.e. use only your own saliva with its digestive enzymes to soften the food in your mouth.

Being full and satisfied means “I don’t feel like eating more” and not “I’ve eaten so much that I can’t swallow another bite”. If you overload your intestines, even the healthiest food will spoil because the symbiotically living microorganisms are unable to digest it. Undigested food begins to ferment within the stomach and intestines. As a consequence, the stomach and intestines lose their cleansing power.

The interval between a main meal and the next meal should be at least 4 to 5 hours.

The healthiest way to prepare warm food is to cook on a wood-fired kitchen stove.

Eat mindfully, i.e. concentrate on eating only, taking small bites and chewing them for a long time before swallowing, with all-embracing gratitude and **without external multimedia influences**, such as daily newspapers, radio, TV and mobile phones.

5.11. Energy follows our expectations

The accuracy of weather forecasts has increased dramatically since the media has reached people everywhere and quickly. In my opinion, this is not only due to advanced technology, but also due to the fact that many people expect the weather to be as predicted. If a hurricane is forecast and expected by many people, it will get even more energy.
There are people who strictly adhere to a lunar calendar when it comes to cutting their hair, sowing, planting, weeding and even cleaning (e.g. their windows). Here too, the energy follows the expectations of many people. If people only follow external instructions (of a lunar calendar, etc.), their instinct and intuition will gradually get lost. I always follow my instinct and intuition "in the here and now", without the help of a lunar calendar and the like. Nevertheless, I harvest many garden gifts every year. Unfortunately, the knowledge that energy follows our expectations is also used by profit-oriented retailers, by profit-oriented companies and by politicians to manipulate and deceive consumers in a very targeted way in order to achieve consumerist behaviour and the desired mass opinions.

5.12. Like goes into resonance with like, and like attracts like.

Have you ever asked yourself why people often experience the same environment or living space differently?
A friend of mine told me about her self-discovery holiday in Croatia in the summer. One of the self-discovery exercises was that each participant had to spend an hour completely alone in a completely dark cave. My friend enjoyed the security and the peace and quiet in the cave and she would have loved to stay there even longer, "shielded from the noisy world outside". Inside the cave, my fried felt safe and (self-)protected because she only went into resonance with energies, vibrations and emotions of the **power of light and love**. Other participants experienced the opposite in the same cave and stopped the exercise prematurely due to intense fears.

People who do not feel comfortable (any more) in their own house because they always go into resonance with fear-inducing energies and thus are scared and have nightmares, often try to remove negative energies, vibrations and emotions from their home with rituals such as fumigation, laevorotatory water, dream catchers, etc. However, such rituals are of no use as long as the **cause of the fears** within oneself, as well as between oneself and beings and life itself, has not been recognised and the personal issue has not been resolved. If the causes of discomfort in one's home are inexplicable loss of energy or flu-like symptoms, back or neck pain, etc., it might be the case that there are sources of electromagnetic, digital or multimedia disturbances in the home.

5.13. Water is a carrier of energy

Many experiments have been conducted with water. Two glasses were filled with water; words vibrating with the power of light and love (love, peace, harmony ...) were written on one glass and words vibrating in a blocking and destructive way were written on the other glass. Both glasses were placed side by side in the same room. The water with the blocking and destructive words on the glass soon turned turbid and smelt like manure. The water with the

words vibrating with light and love was in perfect condition even after a long time. Afterwards both the turbid water and the clear water were frozen. In a frozen state, the clear water formed **incredibly beautiful crystals**, whereas the turbid water was unable to form a single crystal. The most beautiful crystals were formed by water when only two pieces of information of light and love were provided. I am delighted with every snowflake every year because the formation of crystals is proof for me that the water vibrates with good energy and that it can regenerate itself again and again.
The physical or gross body of living organisms is made up mainly of water. (A brand-new human baby is 80% water.) If the water element in beings vibrates with the power of its own light and love, beings are in the flow of being and living that nourishes the power of light and love and where, in the water element, **exclusively love flows freely in a closed cycle**. **In this case, the masculine and feminine forces (kidney and bladder energy) are comprehensively coordinated and in perfect harmony and balance, while nourishing the power of light and love.**
If, in places (environment, living spaces ...) of the being and living of natural phenomena, the water element is in the biorhythmic ecological balance and in harmony within itself, as well as between itself and all elements (water, wood, fire, earth, metal/air), all natural phenomena **in these places** can unfold and turn into beautiful crystals.

In the summer of 2017, I spent some time on Rügen island at the Baltic Sea. Very early in the morning at sunrise, I did my morning exercises on the beach (tapping, meridian stretching, running and swimming). Afterwards I always felt like a new woman and felt ready for my daily activities. Sitting in a forest at a reed belt amidst a nature reserve, surrounded by many ducks and birds, I spent many hours writing this book.
One morning in the forest, my writing was flowing so well that I did not want to stop, even though I was very cold. At noon I rode my bike to the beach to warm up. Since swimming in the sea in the morning felt so good to me, I also swam a few lengths in the sea in the same place at noon after the hot sun had warmed me up. During the night I could not sleep because my energy flow was blocked in the bladder meridian (water element), my legs and hands hurt and I had to empty my bladder very often.

The problem was this: The **water** in the sea, as a **carrier of energy**, had stored electromagnetic, digital and multimedia contamination brought to the beach by beach goers (the beach was overcrowded); at noon, while I had been swimming, the water element within myself (as a carrier of energy as well) had absorbed this contamination from the seawater and from the air. When I got up in the morning, I felt weary and lacked energy. Only the meridian stretching exercises and meditations in the morning helped my energy flow again. For this reason, I rode my bike to quiet and lonely beach places only, without wicker beach chairs and sunscreen and without electromagnetic, digital and multimedia influences.

Water revitalisers / water ionisers

Water revitalisers are not in line with the natural oscillation of water. For this reason, they bring disturbance and disharmony to the water. It is a great advantage if water flows out of the pipes using its own pressure; in this case, the water is not contaminated with electromagnetic waves.
Water ionisers are operated **electromagnetically** and thus are out of the question for me.

5.14. The soul matrix

Life in the material world of physical dense matter, which is perceived as real "in the here and now", is one of many lives. In the world of subtle matter, there are no time or space limitations, but only the "here and now". If the soul of somebody has travelled to one of their lives, where there are personal issues to resolve which have been brought into consciousness "in the here and now", they often have hyper realistic dreams while they are in deep sleep during the night, in light sleep at dawn or in a state of deep relaxation. When I was 12 years old, I experienced for the first time that my soul can leave my gross body. At that time, I could not cope with the level of awareness my mind and soul had without a gross body. Since I less and less perceived my gross body during such soul travels, I was scared of losing my matter. Today, soul travels are an everyday occurrence for me.

As soon as issues and the causes of these issues have been comprehensively reconciled and resolved “in the here and now” within oneself, as well as between oneself and all beings involved in these issues, the **soul matrix** (vibration) will change “in the here and now”. This is because these issues (which are often traumatic experiences with fears and shocks) and their causes have been resolved (transformed into emptiness or into love) “in the here and now” **with the love** residing within oneself, as well as between oneself and all beings and life itself, in a process of self-purification, self-regeneration and self-healing.
Controlled by the soul matrix, souls use to incarnate in families where the vibration of the family system is in line with the soul’s own vibration “in the here and now”. Souls vibrating with the power of their own light and love use to incarnate in a family system that vibrates with full physical, mental and spiritual well-being and with soul, family and world peace.

During one of my many self-purifying, self-regenerating and self-healing processes, my soul travelled to a past life in which my child drowned while I was taking care of her. When I came to myself, I was bathed in sweat, terrified and racked with guilt. In this (past) life, both my daughter and I were no longer in (self-)protection and (self-)safety because at that time, we were living out (self-)blocking and (self-)destructive behaviours in the family system with disharmonies and imbalances of “giving and taking”, **which we wanted to let go of in this life, “in the here and now”**. “In the here and now”, I directed my love towards the cause of “fate” as well as towards me, my daughter and all beings involved in the issue. The love within myself, as well as between myself and my daughter, at that time—the love within oneself, as well as between oneself and all beings and life itself—comprehensively reconciled and dissolved all causes of the misfortune, such as all (self-)blocking and (self-)destructive manifestations, fixations and fanaticism with behaviours that are not identical to the love residing within oneself and with disharmonies and imbalances of “giving and taking”, as well as all addictions, fears, shocks, feelings of guilt, etc. caused by the trauma. And then, “in the here and now” and **in all energy flows, love began to flow freely again in a closed cycle** between myself, the soul of my daughter (at that time) and all beings involved in the misfortune.

It was not long after this experience that symptoms of my body, mind and soul again drew my attention to personal issues to work on. I was working on this book up on the alp in a harmonious environment. My writing was flowing very well and I was completely at ease. In the evening I suddenly got severe pain in my uterus, colon and sacrum. I was very tired and suffering a lot of pain when I went to bed. After I had directed my love towards myself and towards the cause of my unpleasant symptoms, I fell asleep. While I was in deep sleep and in a state of deep relaxation during the night, all (self-)blockages in my energy flows resolved in a process of self-regeneration, self-transformation and self-healing. Early in the morning, "in the here and now", true, wise and knowledge-based information about the **causes** of my symptoms flew, through my crown chakra with the flame of life, from the power source of light and love residing within myself to my self-awareness, my self-perception and my self-knowledge.
"In the here and now", I perceived the causes of the symptoms of my body, mind and soul. Since we did not want to have more children after the birth of our third daughter, I had a copper spiral set (I would never do that again). Although the fertilised eggs were no longer able to implant in the uterine lining, another seven children incarnated into our family system. Since the way to the womb was blocked, these children died soon after having incarnated. So I directed my love towards myself, towards all my children, including the children who were not given the chance to live, towards my husband and towards all other beings involved in the issue for the purpose of maintaining and restoring full physical, mental and spiritual well-being and enjoying soul and **family peace within the family system**. And then, "in the here and now", in all energy flows and in flows of being and living that nourish the power of light and love, **exclusively love** began to **flow freely in a closed cycle** in and between all souls of the family system. The next day I felt neither guilt nor pain.

6.1. Evaluation-oriented influences from Christianity

In Christian religious systems, as well as in many other religious systems, we can find being- and gender-specific evaluations as well as social classifications built on often cruel illusions, delusions and hallucinations that go deep into people's patterns of thought and belief.
People who are in bondage to the Church, repeatedly go into resonance with (self-)blocking and (self-)destructive energies, vibrations and emotions from their evaluation-oriented religious system—energies which will also manifest in their patterns of thought, belief, lifestyle and behaviour within themselves and their family system. This happens especially when they actively participate in Christian rituals, masses and faith traditions.
If people's evaluation-oriented patterns of thought and belief turn a into (self-) destructive (religious) fanaticism that is full of illusions and delusions, people who are caught up in this religious fanaticism and within themselves either want to "convert" people of a different faith or drive these people out of their country or their moral community. The Christian doctrine reports about the crusades of the Catholic Church, the Thirty Years' War between Protestants and Catholics in Europe and many Christianisation measures, also with the help of the military, on almost all continents of the world. During his trip through the USA in 2015, the Pope (the head of the Catholic Church) canonised Junípero Serra for his work in Christianisation measures. The Amah Mutsun, a tribal band of Native Americans, had no understanding for this and Valentin Lopez, their spokesman, publicly denounced the cruel consequences of this priest's actions.

6.2. The "holy" self-sacrifice in Christianity

There are, and always have been, people, such as famous actors or Mother Theresa, who dedicate or dedicated themselves entirely to helping the poor and sick. Mother Teresa, like many people before and after her who served the Church in a self-sacrificing way or sacrificed their lives for the propagation of Christian faith, was beatified and canonised by the Pope of the Catholic Church because of her self-sacrifice for the missionary work of the Church.

More than 2000 years ago, rulers, who often were “gods” for their people, used the fate of Jesus, for which they were responsible, **for their own purposes**. The reason for this is that the extremely poor and exploited people wanted to break out of both poverty and servitude to their rulers and thus were searching for a “God” who would free them from their servitude. As far as I perceive it, the rulers of that time had a “new faith” proclaimed, with the aim of continuing to wield power over the people. Those writing about the new faith had to present the **state of being subordinate and in bondage** to poverty and “God” (at that time, the rulers themselves were the gods) as an **infallible key to salvation of the soul in “paradise”**, so that the oppressed people would no longer be motivated to break out of poverty and servitude to their rulers. To break out of both poverty and the state of being subordinate and in bondage should no longer be desirable for the people who were very poor at that time and **also seeking their salvation**.

As I see it, such events around the birth of Christ were certainly the basis for creating the Christian Bible later on. The writers of the Bible had Jesus come into the world in a stable and in complete poverty. Furthermore, the Bible says that it is easier for a camel to go through the eye of a needle, than for a rich man to enter into the kingdom of God.

The illusion that three wise (i.e. very intelligent and educated) men from different parts of the world also sought their salvation in a **child born in poverty** is another icing on the cake called “Christmas fairy tale”.

In biblical illusions and delusions, poverty, suffering and (self-)sacrifice (for faith/the Church) as well as the **state of being subordinate and in bondage to God, the ruler**, are **presented as an infallible key to “salvation in paradise” after death**.

The Christian doctrine not only “glorifies” the fate of Jesus with a painfully distorted body on the cross, but also presents it as if Jesus went the way of the cross and died on the cross **voluntarily, in a self-sacrificing manner** and for the sake of the people. In a biblical illusion and delusion, Jesus is described as a **being who became God through sacrificing himself** and who is able to **set**

people free from guilt and sins. (This would be a very convenient solution.) In letters of faith we frequently find hidden and open calls to "sacrifice ourselves". Letters of faith urge people to love nothing more than their God. (Note that in former times, the rulers of the people were also the gods of the people.) For me the worst call to absolute obedience can be found in the biblical passage where a father is ordered by his God (the ruler) to sacrifice his son and only child to God (the ruler).
No father or mother (who has an unadulterated, pure and clear sensory perception, intellect and intuition, is autonomous, self-reliant, **self-oriented** and independent of evaluation-oriented systems and has reached a safe harbour) **would sacrifice their child** or allow their child to suffer harm.
The conviction that man is the "crown of creation" and, as such, **has to subdue the earth and dominate it** has served, and continues to serve, as a pretence for many **boundary-disregarding behaviours**, which are increasingly destroying the biorhythmic ecological balance of "giving and taking".

Jesus was a very talented student when he learned the art of healing. Michio Kushi mentions in his book "Your Face Never Lies: What Your Face Reveals About You and Your Health, an Introduction to Oriental Diagnosis" that Jesus was one of the few who, at that time, considered the body, mind and soul as a whole entity "in the here and now" of being and living. Because of his healing successes he was highly appreciated by many people. I am rather convinced that Jesus was not a voluntary victim, neither for humanity, nor for himself or a God. I also don't believe that Jesus went the way of the cross and died on the cross voluntarily and in a self-sacrificing way. Instead, he seems to have been a **victim** of people who were in bondage to the outer world and who were manipulated, remote-controlled and misprogrammed by the outer world when they gave into mass hysteria.
Even Lucifer, who is used in Christianity, but also in many other religions for representations of (self-)punishment and (self-)destruction, is, like all beings, a **being belonging to the power of light and love** because the cause of **all**

beings and life itself is **love**. Representations of punishment and destruction (such as representations of the Krampus figure, the devil, witches and evil beings) in illusionary and delusionary scenarios, but also representations of "good" figures like Superman, fairies, elves and angels are nothing but **illusions and delusions**.

The souls used by religious and other systems for illusions and delusions, including but not limited to Jesus, Lucifer and Mary, are souls like you and me. Like you and I, these souls want to live **"in the here and now", with a free will, in self-determination and freedom, in (self-)safety and in (self-)protection, while enjoying full physical, mental and spiritual well-being as well as soul, family and world peace**. "In the here and now" and **with the love** residing within themselves, as well as between themselves and all beings and life itself, these souls want to **comprehensively reconcile and dissolve** the (self-)blocking and (self-)destructive manifestations, fixations or fanaticisms which are due to **traumatic** experiences and have been manifested—and are still manifested—within themselves in the form of addictions, fears, shocks, mistrust, (self)doubt etc.; the same applies to all behaviours that are not identical to the love residing within themselves and show disharmonies and imbalances of "giving and taking" within themselves, as well as between themselves and all beings involved in issues to work on and life itself.

The cross as a symbol for biorhythm in cycles of being and living

The cross (e.g. a summit cross), **vibrating with the power of its own light and love**, is a **symbol of the power of light and love** for the biorhythm in cycles of being and living, where beings are allowed to live "in the here and now", **enjoying full physical, mental and spiritual well-being as well as soul, family and world peace** within themselves, as well as between themselves and all beings and life itself, in the biorhythmic ecological balance, in the balance of "giving and taking", in a comprehensively healthy growth and in the **flow** of being and living, where, in all energy flows, **exclusively love flows freely in a closed cycle**.

The straight vertical beam of a cross is the symbol for a **strong spine** (healthy back) with a **sense of justice**, truth and equality that is **identical to the love residing within oneself**.

The arms of the horizontal crossbeam point in cardinal directions: e.g. to the east—to the cardinal direction of wood, to the rising sun, to the awakening of spring, to birth (**to the beginning of life**)—and to the west—to the setting sun, to the cardinal direction of metal, to the autumn, where nature collects its forces in its roots and people, when having reached the autumn of their lives, **are in a state of physical, mental and spiritual awareness as well as in a state of self-perception and self-knowledge and realise that the greatest gift in life is being able to let go of the drawn and their own physical dense matter at the end of life, while enjoying full physical, mental and spiritual well-being as well as soul, family and world peace** within themselves, between themselves and all beings and life itself, as well as in all places of being and living, and **while trusting their offspring, knowing that**, in cycles of being and living, **a new beginning in physical dense matter, a rebirth** amidst the diversity of species **is possible again**.

Depending on how a cross is placed, the arms of the crossbeam point either to the east and west or to the south and north. The arm directed to the south points to the cardinal direction of the fire element, to the midday sun, to midlife, to the stage of life where adult children **cut the cord** with their parents and **with systems that are not identical to the love residing within themselves**, in the biorhythm of being and living, **in a self-oriented, completely autonomous and self-reliant way, while being identical to the love residing within themselves**, and, when having reached the peak of their creative powers, build a livelihood and start a family **while being identical to the love residing within themselves**.

The arm directed to the north points to the cardinal direction of the water element, to the silence of the evening, to the winter dormancy and to **finally**

letting go of the drawn and one's own physical dense matter for the next incarnation in the cycle of being and living, **while enjoying full physical, mental and spiritual well-being as well as soul, family and world peace**.

Unfortunately, in the past, especially in the Middle Ages, the cross was abused for death penalties in evaluation-oriented systems due to a (self-)destructive fanaticism built on illusions, hallucinations and delusions.

Together with a painfully distorted body, it became a symbol of self-sacrifice in Christianity in a nature-, gender- and society-specific evaluation-oriented religious system. Wall paintings and pictures in Christian churches, cathedrals, monasteries and chapels, which were built with generous donations from the rulers (due to a fraternisation between the Church and the State and with the tariff penances of people who were **in bondage to the Church**), show splendid representations of illusions, delusions, suffering, self-sacrifice, pain and fear.

Rich people who were in bondage to the Church and a great many poor people of faith who wanted to **save their souls** often gave the shirt off their backs (and also their lives) to facilitate such building projects of the Church.

As splendid works of art and building culture from the respective eras can often only be viewed in such houses of faith, many ecclesiastical buildings became monuments protected by the State; today, these buildings are not only visited by Christians but also by many tourists interested in art and building culture.

In a state of (self-)awareness, (self-)perception and (self-)knowledge, realising that **love is the cause of all beings and life itself** and that **love neither evaluates nor judges**, those drawing **truth, wisdom and knowledge**, in an unadulterated, pure, clear and all-encompassing manner, from the abundance and fullness of the **power source of light and love residing within themselves** disassociate themselves from all evaluation-oriented systems.

6.3. Traditions in village and family life are mostly ecclesiastical traditions

In my environment the influence of the Catholic Church on public life is very strong. This influence is also evident in state-run kindergartens, schools and many educational or training facilities.

Even the seasons are dominated by Christian holidays: The spring by Easter, the summer by Pentecost, the autumn by All Saints' Day and the winter by Christmas. In many countries of the world, Christian faith traditions also determine when the holidays take place in public life during the course of the year. Christmas and Easter are the top highlights of Christian traditions. At Christmas, not only Christian families live out illusions of the Christmas fairy tale from the Bible.

Traditionally, sumptuous, sugary, fatty and denatured meals, which weaken the body, mind and soul and make people lazy (weak), are served on these holidays. This is also often the case when it comes to celebrating or mourning. Even after Christian funerals we traditionally eat roast pork with bread dumplings. At Easter, Christians and their traditional Easter foods (ham, eggs, white yeast bread containing gluten, etc.) receive the blessing of the Christian church, although such a meal is among the most unhealthy eating habits.

These traditional eating habits cultivated on Christian holidays due to group pressure are certainly one of the reasons why people find it so difficult to change disease-causing habits in their lifestyle-related and dietary behaviour, or to distance themselves from blocking and destructive external influences.

Christmas is celebrated in winter—at a time when all beings living in line with the seasonal biorhythm use to hold back (also from eating). During winter dormancy, self-cleansing (detoxification, purification and clear-out), self-regeneration and self-healing are particularly active.

Profit-oriented retailers and profit-oriented manufacturers cleverly market traditions (Christmas, Easter, Pentecost, All Saints' Day, First Communion, Confirmation, etc.) as well as peoples' lifestyle and eating habits, so that their profits are optimised and their influence on people's lifestyle-related, dietary and consumer behaviour is constantly growing. Particularly before traditional holidays, consumerist offers are heavily advertised via multimedia channels in a profit-oriented manner in order to attract consumerist people.

6.4. The fraternisation between the Church and the State is still a common reality

When I wanted to leave the Catholic Church, I was confronted with the fraternisation between the Church and the State, which is still a common reality today. I had to report my wish to leave the Church to a public authority, namely to the District Commission that is responsible for me.
In state-run schools, religious education is still an integral part of the weekly timetable. Parents who do not want to confront their children with evaluation-oriented religious systems often struggle to find a kindergarten or school in their area (especially in rural areas). In a Christian environment, the baptised child receives their First Communion at the age of 7 and makes their Confirmation at the age of 14; this is facilitated by religious education in schools. At Confirmation, the Church has the baptismal vow, made by the parents as representatives of their child, confirmed by the child itself. At Confirmation, the confirmands receive the gift of the "Holy Spirit". This should root the children's lives more deeply in the Christian community of faith, so that the children remain living in bondage and in total obedience to the Church.
Unfortunately, many parents do not pay any attention to the contents of faith rituals. Instead, they focus their attention on the clothing to be worn at Christian festivals, the invitation of relatives and the organisation of the festival. However, despite many influences in their traditional environment, more and more parents and children are distancing themselves from ecclesiastical traditions (rituals).
For me, the worst faith rituals in evaluation-oriented religious systems built on illusions, hallucinations and delusions include circumcision in boys and genital mutilation in girls.

6.5. Baptism is a disregard for the self-determination of the child

Since, in a Christian environment, faith rituals (the sacraments of Baptism, Confirmation and Marriage, funerals etc.) are often strongly manifested in family, social and political systems, parents and their children hardly ever question the texts that are prayed (spoken) and sung during these faith rituals, or the vows (promises) that are made during these rituals. With regard to this issue, parents behave in a similar way as with vaccinations, which they have their children administered without having informed themselves or read the package leaflet beforehand. When a child is baptised, the self-determination of the child is disregarded because baptism (joining the Church) is a decision of the soul.
It should go without saying that children should not be allowed to be part of a faith community before they reach adulthood.

6.6. Religious education in schools has a direct impact on our children's behaviour

A grandmother once came to see me. She was worried because her grandson, a pupil enrolled in the second grade of primary school, did not want to go to school any more because he was suffering from anxiety attacks and nightmares during the night. This behaviour occurred after her grandson had had to write down his "sins" in a religious lesson and since he knew that he would soon have to go to confession. The child was scared because he was taught that all people, including himself, were "sinful beings". On the one hand, he was afraid of a judging and punishing God and on the other hand, he had lost confidence in people.
A client of mine came to see me with her daughter, who also attends the second grade of primary school and is being prepared for First Communion. This girl, too, suffered from sleep disturbance and nightmares during the night. And what's more, she seemed to protect herself from religious lessons with severe skin irritation, loss of appetite and diarrhoea.

The granddaughter of a cousin of mine was no longer able to attend a public school because of such symptoms. This child was released from public school for one year. The child was then taught by her mother and grandmother, who is a primary school teacher. The mother of the child told me that her daughter reacted with fear when she heard church bells ringing. This child is attending a public school again where she was fortunately released from religious classes. So where is the outcry from school psychologists? Why do ecclesiastical systems continue to influence state-run kindergartens, schools and educational or training facilities today?

The director of a school told me that, under Hitler's rule, religious education in schools and the Church Tax Act were agreed upon between the Church and the State (Hitler) for all religions recognised by the State and have been enshrined in law ever since. Since then, the teachers of religion in schools have also been paid by the state. How can it be that agreements made during the National Socialist era are still valid?

Religious instruction at school caused me, too, to experience intense fears when I was a child. When the village priest prepared my classmates and me for our First Communion, we all had to confess our sins to him. But many of my classmates and I could not think of any "sins" we had committed, so the priest recited all the sins we might have committed, such as being unchaste, stealing and lying. He explained to us that it is unchaste to look at or touch "certain parts of the body". If we do not confess these "sins" and do not repent of them (have a guilty conscience), we would have to expiate all our sins after our death in Purgatory. He also frightened us with terrible threats, such as that the Krampus from hell (fear-inducing representation in Christianity) would take sinful children with him. At that time, I reacted to religious lessons in school with anxiety attacks and strong feelings of guilt. I cried for days, holing up and hiding from the Krampus.

When I was in secondary school, I was also confronted with a Catholic priest as a teacher of religion. We had to learn Christian prayer texts, songs and rituals by heart. In the lower grades of secondary school, my classmates and I were afraid of the priest's emotional outbursts. In the higher grades of secondary school, there were often fierce and violent conflicts between him and some cheeky boys. Foaming with rage, he not only insulted them but also slapped them in the face. During these conflicts between the priest and some of the boys, it happened again and again that pupils hid under the table and

he kicked them with his feet. Even though one of my classmates had to be taken to hospital with an ambulance due to a broken nose bone, none of the parents ever dared to question the religious classes or the religion teacher during my school days. The “disobedient children” were always to blame when the reverend freaked out.
My husband told me that he had suffered years of nightmares because of the corporal punishment he had experienced and witnessed during the eight years he spent in a Catholic-run boarding school.

6.7. Fears and constraints related to Christianity

Many of those who have strongly manifested Christian or other religious doctrines built on illusions and delusions in their patterns of thought and belief and in their family system and who actively live out their religious beliefs often have intense fears and feelings of guilt. Self-imposed perfectionism, (self-)punishment and group pressure then often block these people’s lives.
Since they want to meet the demands of faith and of the Church and since they are afraid of a judging and punishing God, of the “Last Judgement” and of the pains of Purgatory, they are often under great pressure. If, **“in the here and now”**, people no longer live with a free will and **in self-determination and freedom** and no longer **live out identity- and individuality-based behaviours that are identical to the love residing within themselves as well as specific to their nature and that nourish the power of light and love**, psychological and physical symptoms, such as pain in the knees, in the back, in the sacrum, in the hips, etc. draw their attention to—externally influenced—(self-)blocking and (self-)destructive social, sexual, nature-specific, lifestyle-related, dietary, consumer and decision-making behaviours that are caused by an imbalance of “giving and taking” as well as by evaluation-oriented patters of thought and belief.

Reincarnation is **“forbidden knowledge”** in Christian circles. Focusing on seeking “salvation” in the outer world, many practising Christians have lost the awareness that dying is a process of letting go of physical dense matter and that human beings (souls) can reincarnate many times in cycles of being and living. Perhaps more and more old people are seeking refuge in Alzheimer's because they are afraid of dying and refuse to consciously experience their dying process.

6.8. Possible reasons why sexuality is often no longer in harmony and balance

A client told me that during her marriage preparation course in 1964, a Catholic priest told the future wives that a wife had no right to refuse a sexual intercourse desired by her husband because the wife was subordinate to the husband. Due to such "acquired beliefs", many men (husbands and bachelors alike) continue to have such expectations in their marital and sexual relationships to this very day. In my practice I treat women and men of all ages who have been unable to explore, experience and express their sexuality in intimate relationships harmoniously and in a gender-specific balance. Several older women confided to me that they had never experienced a sexual orgasm in their intimate relationships, but were regularly faking orgasm, whishing that the sexual contact with their husband would be over quickly. These women had pain and health problems during and after sexual contacts, such as cystitis, irritation and pain in the genital area or in the uterus. If, in intimate relationships, people do not experience and express their sexuality **identically to the love residing within themselves**, harmoniously and in a gender-specific balance, then physical and psychological symptoms as well as disharmonies and imbalances in their intimate relationships will draw their attention to this issue.

Sexuality and sexist representations of the body are marketed in business and social life, especially in the advertising industry, in an extremely consumerist manner. Such multimedia influences are certainly one of the reasons why people no longer live out their identity- and individuality-based behaviours that are identical to the love residing within themselves as well as specific to their nature and that nourish the power of light and love in their social, sexual, nature-specific, lifestyle-related, dietary, consumer and decision-making behaviour. Many intimate relationships focus only on consumerist sexual gratification.

The Catholic Church even gives instructions on how sexuality should be experienced and expressed. In 2016 the Pope (the head of the Catholic Church) once again wrote a 300-page letter, giving instructions to Catholics on how to behave socially and sexually in accordance with the Church's wishes. Although homosexuality continues to be a significant issue (and a subject of silence) in the Catholic Church itself, in this letter, Catholics were called upon for the first time to treat also homosexual and homosexually inclined people with dignity and respect. Since homosexuality was rejected (regarded as a sin) by the Church for a very long time, there is still a negative attitude towards homosexuality in society, which causes many homosexual and homosexually inclined people to conceal, disguise or suppress their sexuality.
Only if people (beings) are independent "in the here and now", in their intimate relationship, with a free will, **in self-determination and freedom**, in a completely autonomous and self-reliant way and **while being identical to the love residing within themselves** in the biorhythm of being and living, and only if they distance and dissociate themselves, "in the here and now", from nature-, gender- and society-specific evaluation-oriented religious and other systems, can the **merging of feminine and masculine forces** on the palate (in the inner energy cycle, where **exclusively love flows freely** in a closed cycle), **be reflected** in their intimate relationship and sexuality, **while nourishing the power of light and love**, while being perfectly, and comprehensively, coordinated, and while maintaining the harmony and balance of "giving and taking".

6.9. The influence of faith in my family of origin

In my family of origin, I experienced physical contact and sexuality in a very contrary way. My mother never hid her body from us. She had a lot of physical contact with her children, which we all enjoyed very much. My father was the opposite. He never showed himself naked to us and there was almost no physical contact between him and his children. I used to hug and kiss my father only on his birthdays.
In the midst of many brothers and sisters and with a mother who was always there for her children, for my grandmother (who depended on her to take care

of her) and later also for her husband (who also depended on her and had a great many fears), I grew up in a large family at a time when my parents were busy building a livelihood from scratch. Most of the time my father was busy building up his company and was often so overwhelmed with work that he was not able to take care of his children and household chores. My eldest sister once told me that when she was a small child, she pretended to be asleep in a cart so that her father would pick her up and carry her into the house; this was the only way for her to get some care and attention from him. In his social and sexual behaviour he was completely in bondage to the Catholic Church. He tried to live according to the precepts of the Church and to meet the expectations of the Church. He was therefore constantly putting himself under pressure and overstretching himself. He tried to get rid of his "sins" and his "bad conscience" (the inner pressure) by regularly confessing his faults and mistakes. Out of fear, he shielded his children from village life, except from the obligatory Sunday mass attendance. Contacts between us and the village community were established almost exclusively through activities within the local faith community. However, my mother, my brothers and sisters and I tried again and again to break out of this isolation. My father could get very angry when my mother chatted with other women from our village or read a romance novel. He expected his wife to focus all of her attention on himself. My brothers and sisters and I had to expect to be punished when we were out with other children from our village or when we played in the yard with "other people's" children. As a consequence of our disobedience, balls we played with disappeared. But he would never beat us. As a punishment, we had to kneel in a corner of the room until we asked him to "be allowed to stand up" again. We often kneeled for hours because it was very difficult for us to ask our father for this. My mother, my brothers and sisters and I did not always have an easy time with our father. He behaved in a very critical, judgemental, restrictive and very dominant way towards his family. During my puberty, I dealt extensively with my father's behaviour or rather questioned it. The causes for the (self-)constriction, the intense fears and the many constraints he was subject to were his patterns of thought and belief and a high consumption of meat.
The Catholic faith was strongly manifested in our family system. At least once a week, as well as on All Saints' Day and All Souls' Day, my mother, my brothers and sisters and I had to pray the Rosary together with him for the deceased members of our family, in order that these souls might be released from their

"suffering in purgatory". Due to facing these intense fears and constraints within my family of origin, I could not believe, even as a small child, that there is a God who punishes, evaluates or judges us or deliberately makes beings suffer.
When I was still practising Catholicism (which was part of my life since the day I was born), my motivation for attending mass on Sundays was my wish to belong to the village community. When I was a child and teenager, I used Sundays to meet peers and friends in the village. At that time, I did not yet pay any attention to the contents of prayers and songs. It was only when I was an adult that I could no longer identify with the contents of the texts, vows and rituals of the Church. Since I had increasingly stronger perceptions and often experienced very unpleasant physical reactions, such as pain, dizziness and chills, when facing manifestations of Catholic faith, I finally left the Church.

6.10. Christian funerals

During requiem masses celebrated at Christian funerals, almost all the talk is of sin, guilt and darkness.
At my mother's funeral, I was very sad because, during the requiem mass, the mourners prayed over and over again for the forgiveness of her sins and guilt and for her salvation from the "darkness". Throughout her lifetime, my mother's soul was always directed towards the sun (towards love); I am sure that also after her death her soul keeps being directed towards the light. She has never been and will never be in darkness.
My mother, who had nine children, was the most caring and loving daughter, mum, grandma, wife and friend anybody could ask for. She nursed her mother and husband for many years until their deaths. She was not only my best friend, but also a great loving grandma for my children. She was a cheerful person, she enjoyed singing all her life and her soul has always been directed towards the sun (the light). Her motto was "Happy is he who forgets that which cannot be changed" (Johann Strauß II, Die Fledermaus). Thanks to this attitude towards life, she was always able to cope with very difficult situations and leave the old behind. The way she lived her life "in the here and now", and the

deep gratitude she felt in her life, despite the limitations of old age, were a special experience for me.
During the requiem mass, the priest asked the mourners to donate money for further masses that would help "purify" my mother's soul. Almost all attendants to the requiem mass, including those who knew, appreciated and loved my mother, immediately reached for their wallets. I will certainly distance and dissociate myself from further such masses for my mother.
Born during the reconstruction period after World War I, she experienced World War II and its terrible consequences first-hand. Her family suffered heavy losses: Her brother was killed in battle and her father was a prisoner of war. When the war was over, she and my father built a livelihood from scratch. I saw her collapse completely when one of her granddaughters died in a traffic accident while she was taking care of her. This was the hardest stroke of fate for our family to endure. Nevertheless, the traces of life engraved in her face gradually disappeared during the last two years of her life. Just before she died, the skin on her face was completely smooth. As early as during her lifetime, my mother was in a state of high physical, mental and spiritual awareness. I do hope and wish that her soul will incarnate into our family system again and that this reincarnation will give her the opportunity to enjoy full physical, mental and spiritual well-being, and will take place in soul and family peace.

Highly toxic gases are generated by the decomposition of any organic matter. Fat from dead organisms deposits inside the earth. Major oil and gas reserves originate from dead dinosaurs and large marine animals.
For ecological reasons I wish my body to be burned after I die, without Christian rites. My ashes shall feed a tree.

6.11. Targeted use of suggestions

Phrases such as "through my fault" and "Have mercy on the poor souls in purgatory" in Catholic prayers and songs, which are recited again and again in the context of faith rituals and faith traditions, particularly during Catholic masses, have a **suggestive effect** that is well-desired by the Church. As a result, feelings of guilt, a guilty conscience, fear, the experience of being in bondage

to the church, etc. will become rampant in people. Texts that are repeated again and again in prayers are formulated in such a way that churchgoers manifest behaviours desired by the Church in their patters of thought and belief as well as in their family system. The prayers of the Rosary have a very high suggestive effect because of the frequent repetition of the texts.
The Church's strategic claim that human beings are born "in original sin", i.e. as sinful creatures, unquestionably serves the purpose that parents, fearing for the damnation of their child's soul, have their child baptised immediately after birth. For me, this is a form of forced Christianisation.

6.12. Undesirable suggestive effects of autogenic training

The consciously controlled manifestation of thoughts and beliefs in one's mind by means of frequent repetition of affirmations or "formulas" (suggestive effect) is also the goal of autogenic training. When reading an instruction sheet for autogenic training, which one of my daughters received in a hospital, I realised that it is impossible to harmonise body, mind and soul with these affirmations.
By repeating the words "I am completely calm" after each step of the procedure, practitioners of autogenic training drift into a passive state of mind. By frequently repeating the words "My right arm is completely heavy", practitioners constantly draw "heaviness" (i.e. blocking and destructive energies, vibrations and emotions, such as magnetism) from the outer world into their systems.
The suggestive effect achieved by these affirmations results in the energy flows—present in the flow of being and living—being blocked to an even greater extent than they were originally. As a consequence, physical and psychological symptoms as well as disharmonies and imbalances in relationships, situations and communication in singledom and coupledom, as well as in professional, business, leisure and social life, will increase or even become dominant.
Apart from that, in autogenic training only the right side of the body is addressed. The left side of the body is never mentioned, but completely ignored. For this reason, as well as due to the suggestive effect, even more

disharmonies and imbalances arise between the right and left side of the body and between the right and left hemisphere of the brain than were originally present. In a state of disharmony and imbalance, practitioners are asked to direct their breath to the heart, abdomen (energy centre) and head (face/sight, hearing, taste, smell; brain/thinking; central nervous system; crown chakra with the flame of life).
In this way, the flow of being and living (where,—when a being **vibrates with the power of its own light and love**—in all energy flows, **exclusively love flows freely in a closed cycle**) and, therefore, self-purification, -regeneration and -healing are blocked. As a consequence, due to the blocked flow of energy, strong and all-encompassing life and root forces, energies, vibrations and emotions of the power of light and love as well as true, wise and knowledge-based information drawn from the power source of light and love residing within oneself are no longer available “online” and “free to the door”.
I recommended that my daughter jog in the forest, avoid stress, do meridian stretching exercises or undergo shiatsu or acupuncture treatment instead of practising autogenic training. In this way, her energy flows would start flowing freely again and her own dynamic powers (self-purifying, self-regenerating and self-healing powers ...) would be reactivated.

6.13. A therapeutic method developed in Austria

In Austria, a therapeutic method was developed which is based on the hypothesis that 50% of our physical and psychological problems, as well as of disharmonies and imbalances in relationships, are caused by genetically inherited patterns, while 30% are caused by patterns instilled by our parents and grandparents, and only 10% are “our own” patterns, which are caused by situations and experiences we face in the “outer world”. The remaining 10% are assumed to have been caused by other people, such as teachers, friends, work colleagues, etc.
During the treatment sessions, clients are asked to let go forever of the “external causes” of their physical and psychological symptoms, disharmonies and imbalances. By massaging the client’s hands, the therapist tries to draw the external causes (blocking and destructive energies, vibrations and

emotions) from the energy flows of the fingers, because it is assumed that unpleasant symptoms, as well as disharmonies and imbalances in relationships, have been caused by parents, grandparents, teachers, work colleagues, friends, etc. (i.e. by the outer world alone).
However, this method does not make clients aware of the fact that they themselves—due to their own (self-)blocking and (self-)destructive social, sexual, nature-specific, lifestyle-related, dietary, consumer and decision-making behaviour that is caused by an imbalance of "giving and taking"—may **also repeatedly draw** blocking and destructive energies, vibrations and emotions from "external influences" (i.e. from what they take, ingest and assimilate, also through their diet) **into their systems**. In addition, there is no search for the **reason why** the client does not **distance and dissociate themselves** "in the here and now" from blocking and destructive (family) systems, such as from a family system involving parents and grandparents that is not identical to the love residing within themselves, or from other evaluation-oriented systems, why they are not following the biorhythm of being and living **in an independent, autonomous and self-reliant way and identically to the love residing within themselves**, and why they do not **take personal responsibility within a (family) system that is identical to the love residing within themselves** (i.e. their own family system).
Those who undergo this therapy will be strengthened in their firm belief that they are "victims" of their ancestors, parents, grandparents and fellow human beings. This is why the tendency to blame others and to look for a culprit in the outer world will only get worse after such treatments. In people suffering from mania, this can have serious consequences.

6.14. Family constellations

"Family constellations" is a therapeutic method developed by a Christian priest. It is also used in modern psychiatry. This method also looks for "culprits" (primarily the ancestors) when people have physical and psychological problems or when their relationships have shifted to a state of disharmony and imbalance. In family constellation sessions, those seeking help are asked, under the guidance of a psychologist, to symbolically return the (family)

burdens of the outer world they have shouldered to those responsible for these burdens (ancestors) in the form of a "package of burdens". This can take place in individual or group sessions.
A few years ago, I myself participated in family constellations session in a group setting. In the last session I attended, I was chosen as a representative of a grandfather (ancestor) and acted as a "channel" for this soul. When the grandson handed over the "package of burdens" to me as a representative of the grandfather's soul, I felt very clearly that the soul of the grandfather (ancestor) was also the soul of the grandson (descendant) who handed over the package. The grandfather reincarnated in the same family as his own grandson, because he wanted to resolve personal issues he left behind in the family system.
Although, under the guidance of the psychologist, the reasons for the grandson's strong feelings of guilt and suicidal ideations came to light, by symbolically returning the "package of burdens" to itself, the soul was not able to resolve the issues it left behind in the family system. The head of the family constellation session did not respond to my perceptions because they did not fit into her "concept".

6.15. Massages exceeding clients' pain tolerance

There is a masseur in my environment who exceeds his clients' pain tolerance when massaging them.
After such a massage, one of his clients not only suffered bruises and pain to the treatment sites for a week, but also severe kidney pain. She could no longer manage her daily work schedule due to pain after this treatment. She was in a tense state and plagued by pain and she had her body in a protective posture when she came to see me. Her entire body was tense and cramped. Since her left kidney could no longer slide over her cramped psoas muscle, her renal fascia also became cramped. That was the cause of her severe kidney pain. My treatment of her muscle fascia under her kidney set off a chain reaction, causing all of her fascial spasms to instantly go away.

Another client's appendix scar tissue, which healed 40 years ago, broke up after she had been treated by this masseur, and the scar kept bleeding and only healed after months.
Both clients have tried such treatment following recommendations from their fellow human beings. However, after these painful experiences, further such treatment is out of the question for them. Do people go to this therapist because they want to be in pain, driven by the desire to punish themselves?
During my healing sessions I experience time and again that only through tender loving care and mindful healing touch can weakened energy flows—and thus self-purification, self-regeneration and self-healing—be reactivated.

6.16. Pilgrims' paths

Christian believers seek healing, salvation and enlightenment on pilgrims' paths or in places declared to be holy by the Church—that is, in the outer world. By doing so, many of these people—although they are actually searching for the love, truth, wisdom and knowledge residing within themselves—distance themselves even more from their identity- and individuality-based behaviour (which is identical to the love residing within themselves as well as voluntary and self-determined and maintains the harmony and balance of "giving and taking"). On such paths and in such places, they often receive even more energies, vibrations and emotions from their evaluation-oriented religious system (which is built on illusions, delusions and hallucinations)—energies which will manifest even more strongly within themselves and their family system.

6.17. The need to flee religious wars

In 2015 the media reported on the persecution of Christians and Jews and on their exodus from their homeland. The terrorist group of the Islamic State is threatening Christians and Jews with death if they refuse to convert to Islam or leave the country.

Many people are forced to flee their homes because their lives are in danger or because they cannot identify with religious wars (i.e. they do not want to fight for such wars). A young man who fled Syria (and later published texts directed against the religious war in his homeland on the Internet) told us that he would have been killed if he had not succeeded in escaping or if his family had not made it possible for him to escape. According to him, the escape itself is often very dangerous because smuggling gangs enrich themselves on those who want to leave their country and seek help from them. Many men therefore flee without their wives and children. Particularly the fathers of families hope that, with the help of aid organisations, they will be able to get their families out of the war zones or that peace will soon return to their homeland so that they, too, can return to their families.
Many refugees, even when granted asylum, continue to face religion-based challenges. Here in Austria, some owners of apartments and houses rent these buildings to the state for the accommodation of refugees. This is mainly for economic reasons. Since refugees are not allowed to be employed in our country and the state's financial support is often insufficient, many of them live in these dwellings in poverty and very isolated from the rest of the population. If they face prejudices in their environment, they will shy away from getting in touch with the local population or asking them for help. We made contact with refugees in our surroundings and found out that many of them did not have warm clothes or warm winter shoes for the cold season. Refugees are often treated as unwanted intruders because of prejudices. Prejudiced and anxious people, instead of forming their own opinions, often adopt desired mass opinions—opinions that are formed with manipulated information spread via multimedia channels.
Due to group pressure, they often act, with strong emotions, as vicarious agents for those in power. Many refugees would be immediately willing to work on a non-profit basis in exchange for the financial support given by the asylum-giving state or to earn their own money on farms, in households, by caring for the elderly and the sick, etc., instead of living in asylum, being shut off from society and lacking employment. It is not so long ago that many of our ancestors were also forced to flee their homes. I know from stories that at that time, many refugees were accommodated on farms and worked there for their food and shelter.

Mother Earth provides a home for all people (all beings), no matter where they are born.

6.17.1. Aid organisations

Many aid organisations use the misery of other people to make profit for themselves. There is a fight for market shares and there are aid organisations which even have a "seal of quality" for donations awarded to themselves.
Christian-run aid organisations are no exception. An acquaintance of mine went with refugees to a clothing market for the needy organised by a Christian charity because the refugees were in urgent need of warm winter jackets. At this market, the price for a used winter jacket was higher than that of a new jacket available in the nearest shopping centre. Many people donate good and often valuable clothing because they believe that these garments will be given to **the needy** at zero cost. After this experience, I was no longer willing to buy goods for this "aid" organisation either. Volunteers stand in front of shopping centres and distribute shopping lists of this aid organisation to passers-by. However, the goods received free of charge will not be passed on to the needy for free.

7.1. Educational methods and expectations

Children should be loved without pressure and without expectations. To develop their creativity and talents, they need enough space in a safe home or in a safe environment outside their home.
Children develop best in family systems in which they are allowed to be just another family member. This should be the case when they spend time in groups—with their grandparents or childminders, in the crèche, in kindergarten, at school or at educational or training facilities. If a child receives too much attention by their parents and always takes centre stage within the family unit, their parents' intimate relationship and family life will lose their harmony and balance.

If children are under too much pressure due to educational measures and expectations, they often behave contrary to the expectations of parents, grandparents and society. They often adopt the behaviour of babies because when they were babies they were loved without expectations. They often begin to wet their pants again, become bed-wetters, put their fingers and hands in their mouth or relieve themselves of the pressures they face by biting holes in their clothes or chewing on their fingernails. Tantrums, loud screaming, nightmares, a restless sleep and not being able to be alone may indicate that your child cannot handle outer pressures any more. Some children react to these stresses by developing symptoms of illness, such as a constantly runny nose, sore throats and ears, bronchitis, asthma, constipation or diarrhoea and loss of appetite. If you observe such symptoms in your child, the first important thing to do is to offer the child opportunities to engage in activities that help them release their pressures and relieve their tension. As a second measure, it is essential to clarify what the causes of such physical and psychological symptoms might be. Behavioural abnormalities in children always tell you that their souls are crying out. When trying to find out the cause of conditions and abnormal behaviour, please also pay attention to whether the child is exposed to electromagnetic, digital and multimedia stresses and whether they can spend sufficient time in the fresh air.

It is also important to look at the lifestyle-related and dietary behaviour both within and outside the family (kindergarten, day-care centre, etc.).

Many parents, grandparents, child carers and even doctors give children sweets as a reward for being good and obedient. Such behaviour is actually a punishment for the child, given that sugar, glutamates, flavour enhancers and the like in sweets are addictive and extremely harmful to health, leading to tooth decay, parasite infestation, concentration problems, etc. **Instead of giving them sweets, reward your children by showing interest in what they are doing and by listening attentively to them while spending time with them.** Children have a lot of fun harvesting fruit and vegetables and preparing life and root force-strengthening organic food together with their parents. Your children will also eat such food with enthusiasm.

Only if parents, kindergartens, schools, educational or training facilities, etc. offer their children learning without fear and (group) pressure, without gender-, being- and society-specific evaluations and with a mindful use of

electricity and digital devices, are children protected from blocking and destructive energies, vibrations and emotions from external influences.
Although two of my grandchildren have always loved to play in the forest and by the stream, they refused to go into the forest with me and my husband when they were 3 and 4 years old. The children were afraid of the big bad wolf, the wicked witch and evil forest monsters after being confronted with frightening fairy tales in kindergarten.
Frightening children's stories containing threats and expectations that are used as educational measures are always counterproductive.
After several reassuring and explanatory conversations with them and by singing a recast version of the German song about Hansel and Gretel, which does not contain any scary threats, we were able to motivate them to play in the forest again.

Translated into English, the original song about Hansel and Gretel goes like this:
Hansel and Gretel got lost in the forest.
It was so dark and so bitterly cold.
They came to a little house made of fine gingerbread.
Who could be the lord of this little house?
Yoo-hoo! There shows up an old witch!
She lures the children into the gingerbread house.
She appears quite friendly, but oh Hansel, what trouble!
She wants to bake him as brown as bread in the oven.
Though, as the witch looked into the oven,
She was pushed by Hansel and little Gretel.
The witch had to bake, the children go back home.
Now, the tale of Hansel and Gretel is over.

Translated into English, my new song about Hansel and Gretel goes like this:
Hansel and Gretel ran into the forest.
It was very funny and not cold at all.
They exactly knew the way to the gingerbread house
And walked across the fields and meadows.
Then they came to the little house made of fine gingerbread,
With poems on gingerbread hearts.

Nibble, nibble little mouse,
Are you nibbling at my little house?
The children shouted quickly,
The wind, the wind and not a child.
Oh, the dear old woman is looking out of the window.
She invites the children into the gingerbread house.
The woman is always very friendly and also very wise.
She always tells the children funny stories about forest gnomes.
After eating their fill of the delicious gingerbread,
The children happily ran home to mum and dad.
There also runs a full mouse
And the song of Hansel and Gretel is now over.

In Austria, parents, grandparents, aunts and uncles like to sing the song "Hoppe, hoppe Reiter" to babies and small children while carrying and rocking them.

Translated into English, the original song goes like this:
Hop, hop, rider,
If he falls, he will cry.
If he falls into the ditch,
He will be eaten by the ravens.
If he falls into the mud,
The rider falls with a splash!

The passage "He will be eaten by the ravens" talks even babies into believing that life consists of eating and being eaten. Instead of strengthening the child's confidence, adults sing to them that they can fall into a ditch.
I have also recast this song for my grandchildren so that it no longer contains any threats.

Translated into English, my new "Hoppe, hoppe Reiter" song goes like this:
Hop, hop, hop!
Horsey gallop!
With its nimble legs,
It runs with (name of the child) over sticks and stones.

If the little horse walks, walks, walks,
(name of the child) goes for a ride, ride, ride.
In a trot, trot, trot
The little horse with (name of the child) runs downhill, downhill.
At a gallop, gallop, gallop
(name of the child) hops, hops, hops in the saddle.

Ease the potty training and other pressures

A very sensitive and attentive mother offered her three-year-old, potty trained daughter a diaper again because the girl had not emptied her bowels for three days. After a few days the girl herself had the desire again to go to the toilet for emptying her bladder and bowels.
Even when potty training children, adults often use methods that put children under pressure (pressure to perform). This pressure to perform often continues in kindergarten, at school, in vocational training and later in working life by constantly having to "prove oneself".

A mother came to see me with her son and only child because he was still bed-wetting at the age of eight. Every evening, she gave a disposable nappy to her son; the next morning, the nappy was always wet. I recommended that, as a first measure, she stop offering her son disposable nappies and instead put a bed-wetting sheet made from natural materials into his bed so that he can learn to control his bladder and let go of babyish behaviour. I also recommended that she make sure that her child can sleep in a well-ventilated room free from digital and multimedia influences and equipped with furniture made from natural materials.

7.2. Children follow the example of adults

Parents, educators, teachers, etc. who live their lives **identically to the love residing within themselves** in their identity- and individuality-based behaviour are the best role models for children. Such people also respect all children in

their uniqueness and individuality. They set clear limits and also respect the limits of the children entrusted to them.
When it comes to childcare, parents and carers do not always treat children with care and respect. Sharing photos of one's babies and small children on the internet (on Facebook and the like) is a serious disregard for boundaries; even more so when these children are naked.
I know of families where small children are sat in front of the television in the morning—during breakfast and often before breakfast. With this medium (TV), children are deprived of the space they need to explore the real world and to express their creativity and talents. Children, especially small children, should never watch television without the presence of adults. Babies and children are best protected from electromagnetic, digital and multimedia exposure in their homes when there are no digital devices there or when they are disabled.
In my shiatsu practice, I was repeatedly confronted with children who were exposed to tremendous electromagnetic, digital and multimedia stress. These children were very restless during the day, suffered from anxiety attacks and nightmares at night, screamed and cried very often and had tantrums. The often very noise-sensitive children no longer felt comfortable in their living environment. Since they were repeatedly confronted with illusions and delusions via multimedia, they were afraid of evil men and women, burglars, monsters, ghosts, animals, etc. Due to these fears, they could not, and would not, play alone any more. Instead, they demanded the full attention of their parents, even their parents were in the same room and wanted to do housework alongside them.

7.3. Motherly and fatherly love

Those who have not experienced motherly and/or fatherly love from their parents or surrogate parents as a child often find it difficult to cut the cord with their parents or surrogate parents and build their own **independent life** in a (family) system that is identical to the love residing within themselves. These people often look for support and recognition from other people rather than finding value and worth in themselves. It often happens that even when grown up, such people continue to be the "good son" or the "good daughter" of their

father and/or mother. In intimate relationships, they expect their partner to love them the same way their mother or father did.
In their intimate relationship and in their family life, their partner often takes on the role of a mother or father substitute. This is because those looking for a mother or father substitute often lack independence and enjoy being pampered by their "mummy" or "daddy" together with the younger members of the family.
Due to an extreme imbalance of "giving and taking" in the intimate relationship and in family life, more and more disharmonies and imbalances arise in such intimate relationships and families over time. Physical and psychological symptoms also draw people's attention to the disharmonies and imbalances of "giving and taking" in intimate relationships and family life.
Only when all causes of—often strong—disharmonies and imbalances in intimate relationships and in family life are comprehensively recognised, reconciled and resolved within the couple or family system, can couples and families find their way to a harmonious relationship while maintaining the harmony and balance of "giving and taking".

7.4. Cutting the cord

In humans and mammals, the process of cutting the symbolic cord begins after birth with the **cutting of the umbilical cord** in the biorhythm of being and living. When issues between parents and their children or between siblings are not yet resolved, the process of letting go of one's parents, children and/or brothers and sisters is often a long and difficult one. If processes of cutting the cord are blocked, then all family members (all souls within the family system) have to go in search of the causes and clear up issues that have not yet been resolved as well as the causes of them, by deparasitising, detoxifying, purifying, decluttering, cleansing, letting go of, resolving, eliminating, deleting and transforming into emptiness or into love all (self-)blockages and (self-)destruction, all (self-)blocking and (self-)destructive (parasite) energies, vibrations and emotions as well as all blocking and destructive occupation and domination by foreign souls within themselves, as well as between themselves,—in a self-convinced, (self-)determined and free manner, with a free will and with the love residing within themselves, as well as between themselves and all souls from the family system. The process of cutting the cord should be completed when a person reaches adulthood, or, at the latest, after the person has found their own family, so that a relaxed and mindful approach to maintaining closeness and distance between generations and between siblings, an approach that is **identical to the love residing within oneself**, is possible.

Young parents who are **independent** of their families of origin and of systems that are not identical to the love residing within themselves **in an autonomous and self-reliant way, and in a way that is identical to the love residing within themselves,** create their own (family) system that is **identical to the love residing within themselves**—in peace, harmony and balance within themselves, as well as between themselves and all beings and life itself, and in the biorhythm of being and living. As soon as they have cut the cord in a way that is identical to the love residing within themselves, they take over all-encompassing responsibility for themselves and their family in a **completely autonomous and self-reliant** way.

In their own family system, which is **identical to the love residing within themselves**, they give their motherly and fatherly love not only to their children, but also to themselves.

But this only works if parents also let go of their children in a way that is identical to the love residing within themselves, withdraw when they have reached the autumn of their lives and trust their offspring.

If, after handing over property, companies, businesses, etc. to the next generation, parents or grandparents want to continue taking centre stage (are unable to let go), handovers will fail because the transferee will be hindered in acting **independently and autonomously** and will not be able to assert their identity and individuality independently and autonomously.

8.1. Personal experiences with my clients

A client of mine suffered from extreme fears of failure and feelings of guilt. Her ex-husband and the father of her daughters had left her for another woman when her younger daughter was 18 months old. Although she had been living

with another man for a long time, she was confronted with extreme, still unresolved emotions and strong feelings of guilt at the wedding of her older daughter. She believed that she had not lived up to the expectations of her children's father and had failed in her life. Even as a child she had suffered from such emotions. At school and also later during vocational training, she repeatedly imposed pressure to perform on herself.
She is the firstborn on an agricultural estate and was rejected by her grandfather because she was not a son. Her grandfather was strongly influenced by the family tradition of bequeathing the property to the firstborn son. She was unable to establish a loving relationship with her grandfather until he died. Since she believed that her grandfather was to blame for her fears of failure, she hated him.
She also told me that her younger daughter, whom she loves more than anything else, suffers from anxiety attacks and nightmares at night and still wants to sleep in the same bed with her, even though she is almost 10 years old. When I directed my love towards the daughter's soul, I immediately became aware that the daughter was the grandfather of the mother in her previous life. The grandfather's soul incarnated where, as a grandfather, it had caused a personal issue with my client, preventing love from flowing freely.
After I had told this to my client, she burst into tears and all the emotions that were not identical to the love residing within herself dissolved "in the here and now" and by virtue of the love residing within herself and existing between herself and her daughter (her grandfather). The all-encompassing reconciliation between these two souls has freed my client's daughter from her fears and nightmares and my client from her fears of failure.

Another client of mine, a young mother, had severe pain in her hips and groin area. She told me that she could not let her little son sleep alone in a room because she was afraid that something could happen to the child. That's why every evening she went to bed very early together with her son, even though she still had housework to do. When I made contact with my client's soul, I was able to perceive the cause of her behaviour in her soul matrix. In one of her former lives, her child was taken away from her shortly after she had given birth to them. My client went into resonance with the love I directed towards her and let go of all the fears that have manifested within herself because of her traumatic experience.

Cysts are almost always the physical expression of strong feelings of guilt. Another client of mine, a mother, blamed herself for her son's mental and physical limitations. She had cysts in her breasts and thyroid gland and eventually cysts were found in her uterus. One Friday, this client came to see me. The cysts and growths in her uterus were to be surgically removed the following Monday. In order to make the truth, wisdom and knowledge from the power source of light and love residing within herself available to my client again, I treated all blockages to her body's energy flow. When the energy flowed freely throughout her body again and also all true, wise and knowledge-based information from the power source of light and love residing within my client was available "online" to her again (through her crown chakra), she became aware of the causes of her feelings of guilt within herself and between herself and all souls in the family system. This allowed her personal issue and all causes of this issue to comprehensively reconcile and dissolve "in the here and now" and with the help of the love residing within herself and existing between herself and all beings involved in the issue. The following Monday she went to hospital to have surgery. But her uterus showed no more evidence of growths or cysts and no surgery was needed.

A friend of my daughter was scheduled for surgery in a hospital because a hardened bruise, which was caused by a fall 15 years ago, suddenly caused severe pain again when sitting.
One day before the final diagnosis was made, my daughter's friend had a healing session with me. There she went into resonance with the love I directed towards her and, by doing so, was able to dissolve the cause of her physical symptoms and the shock of her fall "in the here and now", within herself and between herself and all beings involved in the issue. Not only was she free of pain, but the hardened bruise was gone the next day. At the hospital no signs or symptoms could be found either.

8.2. Some autobiographical notes

When I was younger, I found it very difficult *not* to fulfil the wishes of my fellow human beings (in my family, at work, etc.). At that time, it was not possible for

me to set clear limits and to communicate these limits to people around me clearly and with a healthy approach to maintaining dissociation and distance that is identical to the love residing within myself. My life was a life of serving, conforming and justifying myself.
Caught up in evaluation-oriented systems and perfectionism, I wanted to prove that a woman can easily juggle a professional career and a family life. I tried to be the best mother for my children, the most caring wife for my husband plus a successful business woman. For this reason, my fellow human beings, who appreciated me very much, demanded more and more of me. Despite my strong organisational skills, I often found myself overwhelmed with life. I increasingly ignored my own wishes and, at some point, I was no longer aware of my own limits and boundaries.
I regularly treated physical symptoms such as back and knee pain and recurrent sinusitis with medication instead of looking for the causes of my problems. Only when I was completely burned out did I realise that I had to change my way of life and, most importantly, my attitudes and beliefs. After 35 years of service, I left a very evaluation-oriented profession in which a social conscience was less and less in demand. That was the moment when I started to dramatically change my life. Although I was already 50 years old at that time, I wanted to follow a training course in the social sector. I decided to become a qualified shiatsu practitioner. During the training course I realised that, in this social profession, I could draw my creativity, vocations and talents from the abundance and fullness of the power source of light and love residing within myself. Because my interest was so great, I absorbed the knowledge that was highly interesting to me like a sponge, and despite my advanced age I found studying very easy. I took my exams without putting myself under pressure and without being afraid of them. For me, the training to become a shiatsu practitioner was also my best therapy. After having received the diploma in shiatsu therapy and after having treated 270 clients, I opened my own shiatsu practice. In the exercise of my profession, I set clear limits to myself and my clients right from the start. From Monday to Thursday, I treated a maximum of two clients a day (and three in exceptional cases). Even in the first year of my work as a shiatsu practitioner, my diary was fully booked from January to December by regular clients.

Since I set clear limits to myself and my clients, I had enough freedom to live out the joy of writing, which I discovered late in life. In the same year when I opened my shiatsu practice, my first book was published.
When my body sends out signals (symptoms) or when there are discrepancies between me and the people around me, I immediately go in search of the causes. With this approach and in a state of awareness, realising that love is the cause of all beings and life itself, many personal issues and their causes have been resolved, "in the here and now", within myself, as well as between myself and beings and life itself, especially in the family system.
During a holiday stay on the island of Rügen at the Baltic Sea it was easy for me (thanks the vast landscape there that allowed me to reflect on my situation in a farsighted manner) to recognise and let go forever of (self)-blockages, such as perfectionism and (self-)constriction, that had been manifested—and were still manifested—within myself.
On the island of Rügen I met locals and residents from abroad who live their lives in a way that is identical to themselves, in a far-sighted manner as well as with gratitude and satisfaction, and who can enjoy the vastness of the beautiful landscape and nature in a spirit of gratitude. But I also met people who—despite the vast landscape there that allows for farsighted visions—live their lives in a very valuation-oriented manner, caught up in self-constriction and perfectionism.
The most beautiful experiences on the island of Rügen were the sunrises at 6 o'clock in the morning at quiet beach places without wicker beach chairs. I witnessed these sunrises whilst bathing (purifying myself) in the sea, doing my meridian stretching exercises and running long distances on the beach without effort and feeling light as a feather.
After this stay on the island of Rügen, a big issue in the family system between me and my second daughter resolved itself. In late autumn, without having injured myself, I suddenly got so much pain on the inside of my knee that I could only move around with crutches. So I went to see a knee specialist. The doctor said that my meniscus had jumped out of the joint line and probably had tears, and that my knee needed surgery. This diagnosis was confirmed the next day with an MRI scan.
Since knee problems reflect imbalances and disharmonies in the family system, I went in search of possible causes in the family system. I treated my knee with a homemade comfrey ointment. I meditated again and again upon the cause

of my knee problems and while meditating, I breathed the self-purifying, self-regenerating, self-transforming and self-healing powers drawn from the power source of light and love residing within myself directly into my knee and into the cause of my knee problems. A difficult issue between me and my second daughter began to resolve itself and soon I was able to walk without crutches again. After my daughter had sent me a text message saying "I love you", I was completely relieved of pain and free of movement restrictions. My heart was filled with gratitude and joy when I cancelled the surgery appointment.

I was able to let go of my children in the biorhythm of being and living and with the confidence that they are capable and independent within their own (family) system—**in an autonomous and self-reliant way**, and in a way that is identical to the love residing within themselves. I always have enough freedom to live out my creativity, vocations and talents in harmony with the people around me. The "grandma/grandpa day" with the children of our second daughter, which takes place once a week, and the rare visits of my eldest daughter, her life partner and her son—our oldest grandson—to our home (they live in Vienna) are beautiful gifts for me. I am very grateful when I and my family are in good health and everyone lives happily and in peace and harmony "in the here and now"—with themselves and the people around them. I am also grateful for every day that I can spend together with my husband.

I am touched when people go into resonance with the love I direct towards them, recognising the causes of symptoms and resolving issues "in the here and now"—within themselves, as well as between themselves and beings and life itself.

Annexes:

1.1. Meditation for harmonising the elements

Harmonise, “in the here and now”, all elements (water, wood, fire, earth, metal/air) within yourself, between yourself and all beings and life itself, as well as in all places (environment, living spaces ...) of being and living. Make contact with the elements residing within yourself on the hara line (upper and lower abdomen).
The **water energy** (kidney and bladder energy) is just above your pubic bone; the **wood energy** (liver and gall bladder energy) is on the right side below your costal arch; you can make contact with the **fire energy** (in the primary fire: heart and small intestine energy, in the secondary fire: cardiovascular and triple warmer energy) in the middle of your upper abdomen (in the solar plexus area); the **earth energy** is below your right costal arch (stomach energy) and the spleen energy with the pancreatic energy runs from your right costal arch across your navel; you can make contact with the **metal energy** (colon and lung energy) in the lower abdomen and lung area above your chest.

Lie supine on a mat on the floor, on a sofa or in bed and make contact with all the elements within yourself, between yourself and all beings and life itself, as well as in all places (environment, living spaces ...) of being and living, **clockwise** and “in the here and now”, by placing your hands on the points of the hara line described above, starting with the water. Breathe **your love** into the respective element and imagine that the **love** residing in this element goes into resonance with the **love you directed towards this element** and that the **feminine and masculine forces** are harmonised in this element, **while nourishing the power of light and love**. When you feel a pleasant warmth beneath your hands, you can direct your love towards the next element.
When, in all elements, the feminine and masculine forces are coordinated **in harmony and balance, while nourishing the power of light and love**, place your hands in a circle around your navel and imagine that all elements are coordinated, **while nourishing the power of light and love, “in the here and now”**, in the biorhythmic ecological balance, in a comprehensively healthy

growth and in the flow of being and living, where, in all energy flows, **exclusively love flows freely in a closed cycle**, and that **the harmony and balance is reflected in and between the elements** in all beings and life itself, as well as in all places (environment, living spaces ...) of being and living.

1.2. Loving care is always reflected "in the here and now" because **love goes into resonance with love**

In a state of self-awareness, self-perception and self-knowledge, realising that **love is the cause of all beings and life itself**, stretch out your hands, with your palms facing up, in all cardinal directions to symbolise **the loving care you take of yourself as well as of all beings and life itself**, beginning with the wood (towards the sunrise) and followed by the fire (towards the midday sun), the earth (towards the late afternoon sun), the metal (towards the setting sun) and the water (towards the stillness of the night). Bring your hands back to your body and, while doing so, imagine that **love goes into resonance with love** residing "in the here and now" and that **the love given by you is reflected "in the here and now" within yourself, as well as between yourself and all beings and life itself**. Repeat this exercise ten times.

Afterwards, put your hands up in the air and stretch the right and left sides along the course of the gallbladder energy (the performing energy that is identical to the love residing within yourself) by dropping your hands and head to the right side and then to the left side. Take ten deep breaths on each side. Afterwards, throw your hands up in the air once again and imagine that you are, "in the here and now", in a state of self-awareness, self-perception and self-knowledge, realising that **love is the cause of all beings and life itself**. In this state of awareness, you can draw, "in the here and now", from the abundance and fullness of the **power source of light and love**—with all-embacing gratitude, in a self-dynamic, automated and selfactive way and without consuming any resources. Then go into a squatting position and imagine that you are stable, strong in your midst and identical to the **love residing within yourself**. Finally, stand up, dance, sing, whistle and imagine that you are going through life as lightly as a feather, that you are living "in the here and now" and with a healthy approach to maintaining dissociation and distance that is **identical to the love residing within yourself**, that you can distance and dissociate yourself from all evaluation-oriented systems, that you are **independent, in a completely autonomous and self-reliant way and while being identical to the love residing within yourself**, "in the here and now", in the biorhythm of being and living, in a (family) system that is identical to the love residing within yourself and in the flow of being and living that nourishes the power of light and love and where, in all energy flows, **exclusively love flows freely in a closed cycle** and that **you are sealed with the power of light and love and are fully protected, in (self-)safety and in (self-)protection**, against blocking and destructive energies, vibrations and emotions from external influences.